Epic Fails

Epic Fails

The Edsel, the Mullet, and Other Icons of Unpopular Culture

Salvador Jimenez Murguía

ROWMAN & LITTLEFIELD
Lanham • Boulder • New York • London

Published by Rowman & Littlefield
An imprint of The Rowman & Littlefield Publishing Group, Inc.
4501 Forbes Boulevard, Suite 200, Lanham, Maryland 20706
www.rowman.com

Unit A, Whitacre Mews, 26-34 Stannary Street, London SE11 4AB

British Library Cataloguing in Publication Information Available

Library of Congress Cataloging-in-Publication Data Available

LCCN 201800437 (print) | ISBN 9781538103722 (electronic) | ISBN 9781538103715 (hardback : alk. paper)

∞™ The paper used in this publication meets the minimum requirements of American National Standard for Information Sciences—Permanence of Paper for Printed Library Materials, ANSI/NISO Z39.48-1992.

Printed in the United States of America

To my mother, Olivia,
who taught me in so many ways that wrapped in every failure
is an endearing lesson about one's potential for success.

Contents

Acknowledgments

This book is actually the result of a number of failed attempts at publication. Because of this, I would like to thank all of the previous publishers that contracted the book and then ultimately canceled the agreement. Without their help, I would not have received the much-needed scrutiny that brought this book to the condition it is today. Moreover, by failing to see this book into publication so many times, I was able to locate an ideal fit for it at Rowman & Littlefield. With the help and interest of Stephen Ryan, senior acquisitions editor at Rowman & Littlefield, this book has finally achieved success in publication—for this, I am incredibly grateful to Mr. Ryan. I would also like to thank Dr. Cynthia Miller of Emerson College, Dr. Bob Batchelor of Miami University, and Dr. Norma Jones of Muller Entertainment, all of whom were instrumental in directing me to Rowman & Littlefield.

I received funding for travel and fieldwork from Akita International University, and I am equally grateful for its continued support of my research. In particular, university vice president Peter McCagg and librarian Yukari McCagg were invaluable in offering advice and guidance.

Finally, I would like to express my deepest gratitude to my family—Hide, Koki, Kiki, and Poli—for laughing aloud when I read my manuscript to them. Nothing inspired me more than watching my wife and kids demonstrate that much interest and enthusiasm for my work!

Introduction

In early July 2009, Chicago Public Media's popular radio program *This American Life* featured a story of an individual who claimed insanity in an attempt to avoid a lengthy prison sentence. Explored through the colorful reporting of Welsh comedian/journalist Jon Ronson, the story begins with a reference to an edition of the *Diagnostic and Statistical Manual of Mental Disorders* (DSM-IV-TR), a standard manual of diagnosis used by mental health professionals. His playful articulation running at full speed, Ronson reflects upon his own self-diagnosis:

> While flipping through it, I instantly diagnosed myself with twelve different disorders, including but not limited to "Disorder of Written Expression," which is poor handwriting; "Arithmetic Learning Disorder," which has luckily been cured since I bought a calculator; and "Nightmare Disorder," which is diagnosed when the sufferer dreams of being pursued or declared a failure. All my nightmares involve someone chasing me down the street while yelling: "You're a failure!" I closed the manual. I never realized how unbelievably nuts I was.[1]

The sleep disorder Ronson refers to is indeed found within the DSM-IV-TR under "Nightmare Disorder."[2] In actuality, however, this disorder as explained in the DSM-IV-TR mentions failure only peripherally. Aside from this and other subtle references throughout the social sciences, failure is not somehow bound to any one human shortcoming, which certainly does not suggest that failure is in an exclusive category of its own. Instead, failure, as it will be used in this book, may be thought of in more relative and practical terms: failure is simply a lack of success.

America's many successful inventions over the years—from the lightbulb and the Brooklyn Bridge to Hollywood and the internet—have often been the result of a stunning combination of innovation and ambition. Such successes have been honored as things that have changed American lives for the better, yet just as there are national nightmares that offset the notion of an American Dream, there are also cultural by-products and failures lining the road to America's iconic reputation as a primary contributor to modern civilization. Thousands of memes parodying failures flood the internet daily, demonstrating that Americans love to laugh where ambition has overreached and ingenuity has fallen short. Nevertheless, just because something is a failure doesn't necessarily mean that it doesn't matter.

This book surveys some of the most iconic failures in American popular culture in order to shed light on the inherent, often comic strain in American life between success and failure, fame and infamy: in sum, between what Americans most strive for and what they most fear. Epic fails, as I describe them, are not only the "next big things" but also those more popularly *unpopular* things that get bundled in with major flashes in the pan. From such failed gadgetry as the Betamax and Microsoft Zune to fashion flops like the mullet and Zubaz, this book captures the entertaining milieu of failure while offering interpretations of both the intentions of these endeavors prior to their collapse as well as speculations about their counterfactual position and place in the history of American popular culture.

The aim of this book is geared more toward interpretation than explanation. Although a definitive treatise on failure, its causes, and even ideas about how to prevent it would certainly be a useful contribution to research on this subject, in reality endeavors such as these simply do not figure into the multiplicity of interpretations that I have used to guide this text. Many of the chapters contained herein are steered by well-established research from the social sciences and humanities, effectively offering readers both a case study in unpopular culture and an accessible theoretical model to assist them in arriving at their own conclusions.

Notwithstanding my reluctance to offer positivist explanations, I do make some early categorical generalizations about how these cases ended up as failures. Indeed, at least three broad categories of failure are at the thrust of this book: (1) failure due to negative consumer reception, (2) failure of an endeavor that was doomed from its inception by a lack of vision, and (3) failure occasioned by either poor timing or simply the progression of time that rendered a product or production passé.

To begin, many endeavors fail because of poor reception by the general public. As many of the products and productions of popular culture found in these pages were intended to be mechanisms for generating profit, it follows that customers or audiences vote for the popularity of these endeavors through their choices about how to spend their money. Success or popularity in these cases is thus tied to the positive reception of, or satisfaction with, commercial products.

One illustration of this category involves the reception of a marketing campaign by special interest groups. In March 1989 Madonna released her fourth album, titled *Like a Prayer*. With her popularity peaking among young audiences, the soft drink purveyor PepsiCo brokered a deal to use the first single of Madonna's new album as the sound track for one of its commercials. According to Phil Dusenberry, former chairman of BBDO, the advertising agency overseeing the marketing campaign, the Pepsi-Madonna agreement almost immediately fell apart because of an assumption about connections audiences would draw between the content of Madonna's performance in the commercial and the content of her performance in the song's music video. Although the commercial performance and the music video were substantially different, they were both running at the same time, and Pepsi was concerned that audiences might make connections between the advertisement and the provocative imagery from the video—a potentially controversial interplay: "It was the Catholic and Protestant communities that really howled. The 'Like a Prayer' video was an incendiary, prurient mishmash of Christian church imagery that many people of faith regarded as obscene and sacrilegious. And because the video song was also the Pepsi song, all hell broke loose."[3]

Despite Madonna's popularity, special interest groups—namely, religious assemblies—held enough clout to convince Pepsi that the content of her video

Madonna in the "Like a Prayer" music video.
Sire Records/Photofest © Sire Records

was too alarming for television and that the company should reconsider which celebrities it wished the public to associate with its product. In this instance, the conflict between the content of the performance and the religious values of particular audiences resulted in the failure of the much anticipated commercial.

Another general category is the endeavor whose failure is a foregone conclusion due to errors in manufacturing, marketing, or distribution. Some products and productions fail due to a lack of entrepreneurial foresight, including poor planning, absence of innovation, or even the shortcomings of the creators and inventors themselves. In the late 1980s, for example, the tobacco industry came under siege by antitobacco lobbyists and public health-care advocates. As tobacco industry tycoons attempted to defend against evidence of the negative health effects associated with tobacco use, ideas began to circulate among Big Tobacco about ways to maintain profits in the face of impending public condemnation. Of course, the addictive effects of nicotine ensured a steady flow of revenue for some time, but modifying its image as a pusher of cancer-causing agents would be a much more ideal long-term solution for the tobacco industry.

In 1988 the R. J. Reynolds Tobacco Company introduced the Premier, a product dubbed by the media as a "smokeless" cigarette. On the surface, the Premier appeared similar to conventional cigarettes, yet on the inside, the cigarette was designed to burn "cleaner," using a small piece of charcoal-like carbon that fueled a much lighter and more efficient burn. However, when these cigarettes were test-marketed, consumers weren't sold on the idea. In addition to the 20- to 30-cent increase in cost per pack, customers complained about everything from the taste, smell, and feel to the difficulty of trying to actually smoke these cigarettes.[4] According to one critic, "Inhaling the Premier required vacuum powered lungs, lighting it virtually required a blowtorch, and, if successfully lit with a match, the sulfur reaction produced a smell and a flavor that left users retching."[5]

As negative consumer reactions mounted and trials showed no real increase in sales, the Premier cigarette concept was scrapped after only four months. Yet R. J. Reynolds took another shot at cultivating a market for the smokeless cigarette just four years later, rebranding it as the Eclipse. Nonprofit health organizations and authorities such as the American Heart Association, the American Cancer Society, the American Lung Association, and the US Surgeon General pounced on the company's marketing tactics, which attempted to position the Eclipse as having healthier effects than conventional cigarettes. But just as the Premier had, the Eclipse failed to spark consumer interest.

The third category of failure discussed in this book deals with notions of both time and timing. The simple progression of time can render some products and productions out of style, and regardless of any perceived popular successes they once achieved, their lasting images may be beset by burlesque allusions. The fashion industry, one area of commercial culture in which success and profit are often entwined with changing styles, is particularly affected by time. In addition to the progression of seasons—which requires changes to accommodate the weather and the use of colors that complement nature's transformations—many fashion styles conjure up memories of particular periods in time. Take, for example, the mid- to late 1970s, with such fashions as platform shoes, flared-collar lapels, and polyester pants; or the 1980s, which featured big hair glued together by copious amounts of hairspray, shiny spandex bicycling shorts, and broad upper torsos fitted with draping rayon blouses ever-so-slightly hoisted on bulky foam shoulder pads.

Big hairstyles such as the bouffant and the beehive—generally high-rise tufts of hair stylishly puffed atop the head—evoke an early to mid-1960s look that went relatively dormant for several decades, making popular comebacks—with some variation—in tandem with the rockabilly look, swing, and the jazzy swank of such artists as Brian Setzer and Amy Winehouse. Yet despite nostalgic revivals, when these fashions were in hiatus, these styles were considered simply passé. Fashions tend to ebb and flow, making a given style "all the rage" during one period and "out of place" during another.

In related instances, timing rather than time may set the stage for failure. Where some products and productions tap into the wants and needs of consumers at exactly the right period in time, others surface either too early or too late to accommodate consumer demand—in short, they are, from the start, anachronisms of consumer culture. Technology, above all other cultural productions, is riddled with examples of this. There were the contact lenses from the nineteenth century, made from glass, that predated Kevin Tuohy's "corneal contact lens"—the more modern plastic-like soft lens creation of the late 1940s. There were the rudimentary fax machines capable of transmission more than 120 years before the first machine was introduced commercially by the Xerox Corporation in the 1960s. More recently, the late 1990s were filled with concept technology designed to interface with the burgeoning internet to facilitate communication; the Rabbit phone, for example, could be used at various wireless hotspots several years before the introduction of Wi-Fi technology.

Perhaps one of the most publicized inventions that failed to catch on due in part to its untimely introduction was the electric car. The 2006 documentary film *Who Killed the Electric Car?* chronicled the failure of early attempts to sell the concept of energy efficient and environmentally friendly transportation. Despite the well-received news of this new technology that appeared to be riding the wave of the future and the efforts of an incredibly innovative marketing team to sell these cars to the public, consumers were simply not ready to take a chance on the electric car. Yet as the price of fuel continued to rise throughout the first decade of the twenty-first century, the production—and sale—of cars featuring electric and hybrid technology increased dramatically. In the end, the electric car was technology that failed in its initial run perhaps due to its premature introduction.

Along with these general observations about failure, this book documents some of the more telling cases of unsuccessful endeavors bound to popular culture. Throughout eighteen chronologically arranged chapters, *Epic Fails* addresses failure in such fields as sports, technology, food, beverage, and personal appearance. In the first chapter I discuss how the Edsel automobile became the quintessential example of failure in modern popular culture. With its toilet seat–like grille and other lackluster features, the Edsel became the proverbial punching bag referent for all things that went flop from the late 1950s onward: To be dubbed an "Edsel" was—and still is—tantamount to being called a failure.

In the second chapter I turn to Major League Baseball and the peculiar case the 1976 Chicago White Sox uniforms. When team owner Bill Veeck decided to dress the Sox in shorts as opposed to traditional baseball trousers, the critics came running, capitalizing on yet another opportunity to scrutinize Veeck's quirky gimmickry designed to draw in the crowds. But this was not the only fashion faux pas in sports; in this chapter I also survey other similar uniform failures that run parallel to the Sox's short-lived shorts experiment.

In the next two chapters I tell of the rise and fall of Betamax and LaserDisc, respectively. The former is a tale rife with rumor and speculation about how the proliferation of pornography served to launch the Video Home System (VHS) ahead of the otherwise superior Betamax technology, a colorful example of how failing to be the next big thing may be just as interesting as achieving such success. In the latter story, LaserDisc is discussed as both a pioneer of advanced technology as well as an inconvenient—and perhaps impractical—alternative to the very formats it inspired.

The next chapter moves out of the 1970s and into the 1980s, where I focus my attention on the various combinations of fashion and style. At the forefront stood one hairstyle that seems to define the regally bad look of the 1980s: the mullet. Short in the front and long in the back, the mullet was worn by everyone from the average Joe (and Josephine) to celebrities. In this chapter I detail how the mullet was not simply a hairstyle but instead a complex way of life that ultimately ended in failure a mere decade later.

Remaining focused on fashion and style, the two chapters that follow take up the topics of eyewear and trousers—specifically BluBlocker sunglasses and Zubaz pants. Although the BluBlocker shades survived well into the twenty-first century, their initial commercial marketing was so low-tech and comical, it is considered the "so bad it's actually good" example of failure. Conversely, the parachute-like, neon-colored, zebra-stripe-patterned Zubaz pants characterized a new look in popular culture associated with all things fresh and cool, only to be ridiculed as the ultimate example of kitsch in a matter of years—a funny example of how fun fashion can fail.

In the next four chapters I take a closer look at some failures in the food and beverage industry. After exploring the unsuccessful inventions and marketing strategies of American beverage companies—Coca-Cola's New Coke, Anheuser-Busch's Bud Dry, and PepsiCo's Crystal Pepsi—I then turn to the ill-suited fast-food services of Burger King, offering up some interpretations of how the fast-food giant suffered from a slow-food model. Next I document how consumers saw through Zima, the so-called clear alterative to beer, and failed to drive its market. Rounding off the failures in food and beverage, I tell the story of Frito-Lay's "painfully good" WOW chips, low-calorie snacks that came at a gastronomical price.

In the next chapter I bring the text into the twenty-first century with one of the greatest failures of expectations Americans have ever witnessed: the Y2K scare. With much of the developed world now dependent upon new communication technology made possible by the internet, a rumor circulated in the lead-up to the year 2000 that computers would be unable to make the transition between 1999 and 2000 due to a technical error associated with formatting and storage of calendar data. As the rumor went, without this transition, which would involve everything from personal financial data to more public record keeping, the United States—and the rest of the world—would be thrust into panic and struggle for access to what would become limited resources. Of course, none of these expectations materialized.

In the next chapter I explore the little known political failure of a McDonald's fast-food menu item known as the McAfrika. In 2002, in the midst of growing famine in the central and southern regions of Africa, in particular the Horn of Africa, McDonald's launched its McAfrika hamburger, finding itself embroiled in a host of cultural faux pas that seemed to add up to more than just poor taste.

Next I showcase the incredible tale of the wild, often absurd trials of the XFL, looking for answers as to why such a popular game failed so miserably. Wrapped in hypermasculinity and unapologetic sexism, the XFL took on the National Football League, only to end up as one of the flashiest of flashes in the pan.

In the final two chapters I examine two twenty-first-century failures of material culture resulting from attempts to advance technology. Google's Wave and Microsoft's Zune may have had all the trappings of technological success, but the former was outside of its field of competition, while the latter simply could not compete.

The overarching tenor of this book may appear to berate creativity and innovation at their most critical states of vulnerability, but I do this only in light of the value we may find by celebrating failure. To illuminate how failure can be enjoyed as a cultural by-product of success is to normalize its presence and accept it, for all of its shortcomings, as our own.

In his wonderful treatise on the financial strivings of Americans throughout history and the incredible failures that frequently befell them, Scott Sandage lightheartedly writes that the "American Dream died young and was laid to rest on a splendid afternoon in May of 1862."[6] The occasion Sandage references is the funeral of Henry David Thoreau. The statement, as I read it, is not that the American Dream somehow died alongside Thoreau and his better-world optimism, but that Thoreau's many talents that fell short of common definitions of success somehow established an acceptable precedent for failure. Indeed, in Thoreau's eulogy, delivered by none other than Ralph Waldo Emerson, his shortcomings seemed to invoke a feeling of comfort with disappointment, if not outright praise for a man bound to his free-spirited ambitions. As Sandage adds, "Neither deadbeat nor drunkard, he [Thoreau] was the worst kind of failure: a dreamer."[7] Indeed, the chapters that follow are rife with this kind of failure—the failures of dreamers and the dreams that simply failed.

CHAPTER 1

The Edsel

If you asked someone who of age during the mid- to late 1950s for an example of failure in popular culture, chances are he or she might mention the Ford Edsel, a mid-twentieth-century car that has become a true icon of all things that fail. In fact, among those people I talked to during my research for this book, no other product or production was mentioned more often than the Edsel. Moreover, in the research on failures—popular and otherwise—nothing springs up as frequently as the car with the strange grille. Almost naturally, then, the Edsel belongs in these pages; yet, as I hope will become clear in this chapter, the failure of this automobile may only be superficial, having nothing to do with mechanics or even consumer reception. Instead, when one takes the time to read up on the topic, it is clear that most of the criticism about the Edsel was based upon perceptions of a car that wasn't even around long enough to be experienced by the critics who painted such a poor picture of the vehicle; that is, the Edsel's lifeline was actually cut long before it established itself as the failure for which it is known today.

Nevertheless, it should also become clear that a failure is a failure—no matter to what extent or for what reason—once it has been labeled as such. Similar to the way in which individuals who experience public disrepute have incredible difficulty reinventing their images in a way that is favorable to public standards, so may be the case for items of material culture.

One of the more celebrated historians of American automobiles, Thomas E. Bonsall tells perhaps the most detailed story of the Edsel in his 2002 book *Disaster in Dearborn: The Story of the Edsel*. About the Edsel, Bonsall remarks,

> This is a story that has continued to fascinate people as few other epic disasters in modern history. Certainly few cars have grabbed

the public's fancy as much as the ill-fated Edsel—the *Titanic* of automobiles—a marketing disaster whose magnitude has made it a household word. Indeed, for a parallel one must go back to the *Titanic* itself, which sank in 1912. Both have become metaphors for overweening management ambition and shortsightedness—or worse.[1]

Like Bonsall, many other historians have noted the realities of the Edsel's failure, but at the same time have also suggested that it did not fail on its own, and such a failure like this is far more complex than one might assume.

To truly understand the story of the Edsel, one has to track back in history to the time just after World War II, when Ford was on the rebound from more than a decade of declining sales. Ford's major obstacles to increasing sales were not car designs, but rather organizational structures that held it back from competing with the success of General Motors. In contrast with Ford, General Motors had a multidivisional structure that allowed for, among other things, a more focused delegation overseeing each division, rather than centralized management of all divisions.

After taking the reins of the company from his ailing grandfather, Henry Ford II made the decision to hire as consultants a group of ten former military men who had proven records as statisticians during World War II.[2] With help from this new team, referred to as the Whiz Kids, the Ford Motor Company overhauled its organizational structure, putting new cost controls into place and implementing new manufacturing systems intended to establish further efficiency in the assembly process.

The unforeseen troubles at Ford began with the overhaul and remodeling of its divisional structure. Ford separated the Lincoln-Mercury lines into two separate divisions and added a third division to house the new line for the Edsel. Although the restructuring seemed ambitious, at a cost of more than $480 million, the overseers of the change may have held back some skeptical reservations. The whole move seemed, in a word, risky.

In addition to undertaking a costly reorganization, Ford went to great—though perhaps futile—lengths to capture a profile of its target customers' interests and needs. Mulling over sales strategies for the Edsel, Ford's marketing research director, David Wallace, commissioned research on car psychology. Convinced that the image of an automobile, not necessarily the quality of it, was a major selling point, Wallace advanced the notion that mismatches between image and consumer preferences could amount to real deal-breakers. With this reasoning, Wallace sought to invent an automobile personality that was "vague and protean,"[3] as to avoid such a clash between personality and product.

In another commercial drive, the Edsel team also entertained the public by underwriting an hour-long television special featuring a star-studded cast that included Bing Crosby, Louis Armstrong, Frank Sinatra, and Rosemary Clooney—subtly pushing the automobile's status on unassuming consumers. In this way, the Edsel was the "first-ever attempt to combine modern psychology, marketing-research techniques, and mass media in an elaborately orchestrated campaign to create an instant sensation."[4]

When the Edsel was finally introduced on September 4, 1957—then dubbed "E-day"—the interest of automobile aficionados had been piqued. Marketing strategies that released carefully measured tidbits about the car built excitement and anticipation, drawing the attention of millions across the country. Ford's advertisements had suggested that consumers would see something they had never seen before, and on E-day Ford definitely hit its mark. Yet this wasn't necessarily a good thing: to the surprise of most, the Edsel's looks rather defied expectations.

In contrast with the futuristic spaceship-looking automobiles that were in vogue at the time, the Edsel was a car that seemed to be moving backward in time. No wing-like back end panels like those running rampant among Chevy's 1957 models, or even Ford's then–luxury line, the Lincoln, which had panels that looked ready for flight! Instead, the Edsel's rear end was rather modest and flat looking.

The front end didn't exactly smack of the future, either. In stark contrast to many grilles that looked like wild animal teeth ready to eat up the road ahead of them, the Edsel had an egg-shaped grille. Indeed, above all other features that made the Edsel stand alone—not necessarily due to some extraordinary achievement—was this oval-shaped vertical grille. As Bonsall puts it, "The grille was quickly dubbed the 'horse collar' grille by many. Others, less complimentary, said it looked like a toilet seat or, worse, like a part of the female anatomy. Within the industry, it was described as looking like 'an Oldsmobile sucking a lemon.'"[5]

Notwithstanding the oddities of the car's outer appearance, the inside wasn't so bad. In fact, there were some rather interesting innovations among its interior, including automatic transmission buttons located in the center of the steering wheel, an advanced system for manually lubricating the chassis, a host of state-of-the-art warning features, and, of course, a monster V8 engine. However, one would have to actually test-drive or own an Edsel to get a real appreciation for these innovations. Ultimately, the first impression—its appearance—had to sell the car, and the Edsel's did not.

Yet despite any of these shortcomings—or even all of them in combination—the real reason the Edsel failed had to do more with the changes in Ford's corporate structure than with anything else. These changes, according to business history

Perhaps the most frequently parodied feature of the Edsel is its oval-shaped grille—mocked as resembling everything from a toilet seat to various parts of the human anatomy. ©*iStock/Kalulu*

professor Tom Dicke, meant changes to Ford's overall corporate strategy that simply didn't support the Edsel.[6] As Dicke explains,

> Given that Ford's Executive Committee shifted their strategy before they introduced the Edsel, and they did so because they considered the program unnecessary, not because they believed the car would be unpopular, the Edsel's status as an icon of failure is undeserved. In actuality the Edsel is most accurately remembered not as a product of failure but as a powerful example of the potential hazards of strategic waffling.[7]

Rather than the far more interesting tale of a car that was hit with an ugly stick, the lackluster story of corporate restructuring and strategy modification ultimately made up the bulk of this failure narrative. The details nonetheless merit at least some explanation.

At the top of Ford's list of strategic changes was the diversification of products. In addition to the Ford, Lincoln, and Mercury lines in which Ford was well invested, the company decided to create the new Edsel line with a dedicated division to support it. This was a move that was both risky and costly, with a big emphasis on the latter. Nonetheless, Ford made the changes, spent the money, and reorganized—and some unanticipated events threw a wrench in the machine. According Dicke, Lewis Crusoe, the individual in charge of all automobile production and big supporter of the divisional changes (including Edsel movement) suffered a heart attack just prior to the new car's launch, leaving Ford indefinitely. To complicate matters, the Mercury had yielded such poor sales early on that some dealers were losing money. Moreover by relinquishing these dealers' Lincoln models as a result of rearranging the organization of company divisions and the anticipation of a new competitor born of their parent company, this whole new system was crumbling on the eve of the Edsel's launch.[8] To mitigate some of these issues, Robert McNamara, who replaced Crusoe as executive vice president of production, merged Lincoln and Mercury back into one division, then waited for the Edsel to slowly see its way into the history books.

According to Dicke, these often ignored facts change the discourse on Edsel's failures to one wherein Ford—not consumers—made the choice to terminate a line that wasn't a fit in the coming structural changes it had planned for itself. Dicke's argument is compelling. His research is thorough, and his view of the failure of the Edsel as a result of managerial maneuvers merits quite a bit of attention. Yet does such an excavation of historical narratives lessen the impact of the image of the Edsel as a failure? Regardless of the causes of a particular failure, years of banter and character assassination associated with the failure still remain.

In the end, the reality surrounding the failure is simply real—it was indeed a failure. To better understand how this reality can play out, it's important to view the Edsel's circumstances through a sociological perspective. In the subdiscipline of sociology known as *deviant behavior*, a prominent theoretical approach referred to as *labeling theory* is often used to describe the social construction of deviance. In this perspective, deviant behavior is viewed as a result of attaching negative labels to individuals; these labels may create a self-fulfilling prophecy in which the labeled individual must negotiate, and at times even assume, the overall image the label implies. In other words, deviance is not an inherent feature of individuals that partake in a given behavior, but instead it is a community's disregard of either the individual or the behavior—and the application of labels that reflect this disregard—that generates the deviance as such.

The sociologist Howard S. Becker may have made the most important contributions to this theoretical approach in his research on marijuana users and jazz musicians. Delineating how neither of these groups actually deviate from societal norms, but instead are labeled as doing so, Becker demonstrated a real arbitrariness associated with deviant behavior. As Becker notes,

> Social groups create deviance by making rules whose infraction creates deviance, and by applying those roles to particular people and labeling them as outsiders. From this point of view, deviance is *not* a quality of the act the person commits, but rather a consequence

of the application by others of rules and sanctions to an "offender." The deviant is one to whom that label has been successfully applied; deviant behavior is behavior that people so label.[9]

This presents the argument that individuals can be naturally deviant with a considerable challenge, and this rethinking of environmental circumstances versus biological factors changed the ongoing debates over race, gender, and sexuality. Moreover, the fact that labels and the powers that they wield could be questioned in this light meant that a number of perceived truths merited serious reconsideration. As such, labeling is something that cannot be ignored.

To further illustrate this point, let's take an example of a young woman in high school, well within the throes of adolescence. Perhaps she's attractive and rather likable, both of which generate some exceptional attention from her peers. Although she is quite innocent with regard to relationships, never dating and only subtly taking romantic interest in others, a group of young men begin to objectify her sexually, disseminating rumors that suggest she has strong promiscuous tendencies. Labels like *slut*, *whore*, *easy*, and the like are whispered

Where were you in '62? Maybe stuck driving an Edsel, like Steve (Ron Howard) and Laurie (Cindy Williams) in *American Graffiti* (1973). *MCA/Universal Pictures/Photofest © MCA/Universal Pictures*

about her until finally this young woman learns of these rumors. Emotionally devastated and certainly willing to refute these claims, she is unable to do much of anything about them, as they have spread too rapidly and too far, even reaching students that never actually met her.

Although these rumors are false, the reality for this young woman is that these labels have already been placed upon her, and from this point on she'll have to negotiate a new image in the face of such lies. The passing of time may serve to reduce the attention paid to her now-tainted image, but the damage, for all intents and purposes, has been done.

If one were to take this hypothetical case several steps further, one might also see how easy it would be for such labels to resurface within the young woman's self-consciousness during future occasions involving sex. Perhaps the exploration of her own sexuality may be affected by these labels, causing her to refrain from various activities lest she be relabeled as she had been during her adolescence. Or, conversely, knowing full well that she's already been labeled, she may carelessly engage in promiscuous sexual activity beyond what may be healthy.

Of course, all these hypotheticals seem rather generic and perhaps at first glance even inapplicable to an automobile's image, but the point is that it can be difficult to distance oneself from labels. What the young woman in this example may have going for her is the opportunity to manage the fallout from her labels; an automobile or any inanimate object would not. As difficult as it may be, humans generally have the capacity to repudiate false claims, whereas products simply cannot.

Business marketing professors Pam S. Ellen and Paula F. Bone have advanced this argument, focusing on the labels that adhere to genetically modified (GM) foods. According to Ellen and Bone, "[S]tigma can significantly affect marketplace efficiency by reducing demand for a stigmatized product or service or by inflating demand for those products or services that do not have the stigmatizing mark."[10]

In their 2008 study, Ellen and Bone surveyed 210 potential customers about their attitudes toward different product labels referencing genetic modifications, which have evoked certain stigmas about health risks. Ellen and Bone then presented one of four labels stating that the product was (1) "GM-denied," indicating that the product contains no GM ingredients; (2) "unqualified-GM," an indication of modification that gives explanation for its modification; (3) "qualified-GM," a label indicating modification, but only for the purposes of reducing pesticides; or (4) "GM-yield," indicating modification, but for the purposes of increasing product yield.[11] Responses to these labels revealed something about how perceived stigmas can alter the success of a product.

In contrast to research that shows no negative effects associated with genetic modification, Ellen and Bone found that labels indicating that a product contains GM ingredients increased consumers' negative assumptions about its risk—an indication that the stigma persisted, despite evidence to suggest otherwise. Yet what was more interesting for the purposes of this chapter, and in line with sociological interpretations of labeling theory, was that those labels that state that GM ingredients were *not* present also led to negative beliefs and assumptions about the GM process. In this way, the label itself, not the actual product, perpetuated a negative stigma. In other words, just the presence of a preconceived notion about a label, regardless of what it is intended to convey, is enough to conjure up negative perceptions.

The long and symbolically painful road of humorous jabs and put-downs that the Edsel has traveled since E-day is not unlike the one faced by genetic modification and a host of other processes and products. Audience perceptions are an important, if not central, part of the consumption process, but to view them as the result of rational thought, well-researched investigations, or even scientifically grounded experiments is at best delusional. Instead, the reality is that audience perceptions are quite vulnerable to any number of tenuous factoids, or often irrelevant information that is incorrectly perceived as factual. Indeed, it's this impressionability that marketers are so keen on manipulating, and therein lay the tricks of such a trade.

There has been no shortage of malicious swipes directed at the Edsel in the decades since its inception, but the automobile lacked the human support necessary to massage the stream of ridicule. Dicke's research tells why there was no one there to foster this support, but the years of negative labeling suggests that there is no question about the Edsel's failure in the minds of consumers. If it had failed due to dangerous mechanical missteps that led to serious violations of safety standards, or perhaps some ominous reports of child labor exploitation in its production, then the Edsel would certainly be more deserving of such a consistent campaign of disrepute. Yet its only real failure was that there was no spokesperson present and charged with fielding criticism, as is often the case with products during their introductions. Instead, the Edsel, already buried in the annals of automobile history, was posthumously hit with the barrage of witticism, and in this way, the stigma of failure has simply stuck.

CHAPTER 2

Athletic Uniforms

On July 12, 1979, Steve Dahl, a DJ at Chicago's WDAI, led Disco Demolition Night in Comiskey Park during the intermission of a double-header between the Chicago White Sox and the Detroit Tigers. Billed as a gimmicky marketing stunt in defense of rock music, the event featured a discounted admission price of 98 cents for fans who brought in a disco record for Dahl to ceremoniously destroy. The mixture of alcohol (and the suspected presence of other drugs) with a playful disregard for disco had the crowd poised for destruction right up to Dahl's grand entrance wearing a combat helmet and army fatigues. According to one account, "After leading the crowd in yet another 'Disco sucks!' chant, Dahl detonated the mound of records, blasting shards of flying vinyl all over the park—and sending thousands of wasted kids tumbling out of the stands and onto the field in ecstatic celebration."[1]

With the field too damaged to play on, the White Sox were forced to forfeit the second game to the Tigers. Several dozen fans were arrested and still more were hospitalized. In the end, the "Death of Disco," as it is often referred to, went down as one of the most chaotic events in the history of professional sports. That night, baseball was a mere second to the events of Disco Demolition Night.

Why would secondary commercial events of a marketing gimmick be allowed to disrupt—if not usurp—the primary focus of professional athletic competition? Perhaps the display of wild fandom was just what Major League Baseball (MLB) needed to bring it up to par with the rowdy experience of attending hockey, rugby, soccer, and football games. Yet MLB already had its modest share of similar events, including bloody bench-clearing brawls and beer riots.

Another explanation may have been that the Disco Demolition Night event spiraled out of control due to fan frustration over the poor performance of the White Sox during the 1979 season. But if that were the case, why don't these wild occasions arise every year in ballparks of losing teams across the country—after all, there a host of teams experience bad seasons every year.

Another way of looking at what took place that night in July 1979 is as a crisis of popular expression, a condition whereby the world of popular culture collided with the loosening structure of organized sports. If this were the case, what types of factors might have led to the attenuation of such structures? In this chapter, I argue that in societies that have undergone advanced industrialization, sports are rife with a condition known as *conspicuous leisure*,[2] which can materialize through expressions that emphasize a state of being in repose or nonproductive activity. It is in this way that structures allow for some rather unusual behavior; in sports this often includes experimental marketing and innovative changes to the game. In 1970, for example, Oakland A's owner Charlie O. Finley upped the flashy ante on opening day with the introduction of gold bases.[3] Though they were certainly a dazzling spectacle, the bling-bling bases were soon banned from Major League Baseball.

Team uniforms can be another vehicle for this expression of conspicuous leisure. The uniform's appearance and symbolism—and even its perception as a success or a failure—provide a canvas upon which this type of leisure may be painted. The 2011 University of Maryland Terrapins, for example, added a dash of state pride by incorporating swatches of Maryland's black-and-yellow-checkered state flag into its uniforms. Sports fans and writers alike were quick to criticize the change, which looked like a mishmash of crime scene tape on the mostly white-and-red uniforms. The trend over the last decade or so for professional athletes to don so-called throwback uniforms are often nostalgic for the fans, but just as often result in fashion disasters.

Notwithstanding these more recent examples, at no point in history was this kind of leisurely expression more apparent in sports than during the 1970s. Admittedly partial to the wild era of America and its sports during that decade, Dan Epstein eloquently documents the dazzling world of baseball's funky past in his 2010 book, *Big Hair and Plastic Grass*. As he notes,

> Back then, I thought the Oakland A's green-and-gold uniforms were groovy, not garish; ditto for the Houston Astros' "tequila sunrise" jerseys. I still prefer the sleek, form-fitting look of '70s double knits to the softball tops and pajama bottoms so prevalent in the early twenty-first century, and I still think players who wear long hair, villainous mustaches, bushy sideburns and voluminous Afros look way cooler than those who don't. I can't help it; I'm a child of the '70s.[4]

Although the innovation of personal expression was quite interesting, the decision about what could be worn didn't rest with the players themselves, but rather from the upper echelons of management.

On August 8, 1976, the Chicago White Sox hit the field in Comiskey Park sporting black double-knit polyester shorts and collared jerseys. Rather than the traditional baseball trousers worn by ballplayers for decades, the White Sox came to play in tight shorts and flappy ruffs. Some speculated that the owners of the White Sox—nineteen games back from first place—were looking to attract whatever surge in fan attendance it could get, even if it came at the expense of a few laughs.

At the time, White Sox owner Bill Veeck and his wife, Mary Frances, made a pragmatic case for these outfits, arguing that the new uniforms weren't just a marketing tool, but a way to keep the players cool in the summer heat of Comiskey Park.[5] But Veeck, in typical form, also remarked that the uniforms were more than just practical; they were also a fashion statement:

> We are adding elegance to baseball styles. We may not be the greatest team in baseball, at least not for a few years, but we'll immediately be the most stylish team in the game. The White Sox are not going to be dressed like a bunch of peacocks. There is a difference between color and elegance . . . between style and class. You will be awed. Comiskey Park will replace Paris and New York as the fashion center of the World.[6]

Somewhere in these visions of cultural grandeur, Veeck's colorful personality shone through, and even though the new uniforms appeared to be little more than a publicity stunt, their debut was a telling indication of just how much the notion of leisure was being acted upon in organized sports. Above all the other oddities that emerged during the '70s in baseball, shorts appeared to bring the look of leisure to the foreground of athletic imagery, where the discomfort of hard work could now be ameliorated by casual garments. Yet such imagery was only a flash in the pan, as the White Sox would sport the uniforms only twice more before permanently hanging them up.[7] The uniforms had, in a word, failed.

Two decades after the short-lived short uniforms appeared in Major League Baseball, a new and equally quirky look emerged in college basketball. In 1996, athletic uniforms underwent yet another interesting transformation with the introduction of denim—yes, denim, as in blue jeans. When the durable pants from Levi Strauss & Co. began to circulate in the mid-1870s, it's doubtful that Strauss or his tailor, Jacob Davis, could have imagined that one day there would be a market for their product in college athletics. Yet more than a century later the University of Kentucky Wildcats made denim a central feature of their game day appearances.

In 1966, during one of their several championship-winning seasons, the Wildcats, a major NCAA powerhouse, donned blended denim outfits for both

Shortly before the 1976 season, five retired MLB players modeled the latest uniforms for the Chicago White Sox: Bill "Moose" Skowron, Mo Drabowski, and Jim K. Rivera are all the rage in home hot-weather uniforms, while Dave Nicholson and Dan Osinski look smart in their road uniforms. Chicago White Sox fashion designer—er, owner—Bill Veeck (middle) shows his approval. *Associated Press*

their game and warm-up uniforms, even including traces of the fabric in their high-top sneakers. According to the Converse press release,

> Cons Blue, designed specifically for the [Kentucky] Wildcats, incorporates denim accents into both the uniform and shoe design. The uniform features authentic blue denim panels to contrast the white mesh inserts on the tank and the short. On game day, the Wildcats will also debut a denim trimmed shooting shirt and warm-up suit developed exclusively for the team. In addition to an authentic uniform and shooting shirt, Converse will offer a replica uniform as well as branded Cons Blue for retail sale.[8]

For athletes competing in these uniforms, the idea of sweat accumulating in denim clothing—and the weight factor alone—must have been a discouraging if not uncomfortable thought. Yet with twenty-first-century fashion hindsight, the denim look is certainly revealing of a period when jeans were ubiquitous: a period when everything from denim shorts, long-sleeve button-up shirts, and even fanny packs were everywhere—even on the basketball court. At that point, popular fashion had entered college basketball in a big way, allowing for athletes to express their fashion sense not only off the court, but on it as well. Nonetheless, like the uniforms of 1976 Chicago White Sox, the Wildcats' denim attire failed to appear again after the year they were introduced.

So what can one make of these uniform failures? Those who approved them—like Bill Veeck, in the case of the Chicago White Sox shorts—certainly demonstrated that they had vision, although perhaps not the kind of vision fans were willing to accept. Or perhaps these uniforms were simply signs of their times, short-lived innovations that didn't hold up in the long run. Maybe they can even be viewed as the charming vestiges of an bygone era, leftover icons of nostalgia that tout the way things were. Yet, in my interpretation, there has to be something else.

At the turn of the twentieth century, American sociologist Thorstein Veblen wrote about similar phenomena in the tendencies of what he called the *leisure class*. In his 1899 book *The Theory of the Leisure Class: An Economic Study of Institutions*, Veblen argued that the class divisions that were so well sewn into the social fabric of early modern societies had extended into modern societies in an important way. For Veblen, these class divisions were visible through the upper classes' tendency to showcase their wealth by appearing leisurely, presenting an image of one who does as little as possible in terms of labor. Leisure can be thought of as nonproductive work—literally, work that does not produce anything useful. Thus, one who engages in such leisure is supposed to appear as if he or she is doing nothing, yet receiving or achieving substantially in return. With this, the notion of leisure underwent a growth spurt through the conspicuous display of having time on one's hands, carefree attitudes toward responsibilities, a seemingly natural and effortless accumulation of wealth and resources, and the outright waste of goods and services.

When viewing the dynamics of leisure, Veblen identified mechanisms through which class stratification emerges. Similar (though not exactly identical) to an evolutionary schema, the survival of one class depends on the distinction it can establish between itself and another. Veblen loosely refers to this as *invidious distinction*, or symbolic actions that evoke resentment between individuals: "Invidious comparisons tend to be made between people on the basis of their efficiency in doing work. As a result, people seek to make their efficiency visible to others so that they may gain esteem and be emulated by others."[9]

As these newly differentiated classes become more and more divergent, one mechanism for establishing such distinctions is private ownership or personalized property.[10] The way in which such private ownership is handled and the means by which personal property is treated become part of a public display that conveys one's success and affluence to the surrounding world.

The world of organized sports is not exempt from this; in fact, Veblen mentions sports in this developmental schema, although only in a limited fashion and certainly not directly referencing modern sports. In explaining how certain classes separate from each other based upon the distinctions of industry and business, Veblen notes the nominal titles that are apportioned to those upper classes:

> If there are several grades of aristocracy, the women of high rank are commonly exempt from industrial employment, or at least from the more vulgar kinds of manual labor. The men of the upper classes are not the only exempt, but by prescriptive custom they are debarred, from all industrial occupations. The range of employments open to them is rigidly defined. . . . These employments are government, warfare, religious observances, and sports.[11]

If through inference, however, we extend Veblen's line of reasoning to include the nuances of athletes' performance and even their appearance, we may more easily view examples of this type of conspicuous leisure in full flux.

In organized sports, especially those sports that are showcased through popular media, athletes participate regularly in this form of conspicuous leisure. Once they have made it to the collegial or professional level, it is quite common for athletes to demonstrate separation from their more average peers by modifying their demeanor during play, appearing casual almost to the point of unathletic. Perhaps one the easiest ways of demonstrating this is to blur the boundaries between one's personal life and one's profession. For example, baseball star Manny Ramirez wears loose-fitting shirts, baggy jeans, and long hair off the field, then carries that look onto the field, blurring the line between these two distinctive worlds and conveying to onlookers that he is relaxed and comfortable as he—seemingly effortlessly—earns millions of dollars a year.

When the 1976 White Sox and the 1996 Wildcats introduced their novel uniforms, they may not have been motivated by the same type of personal expression Ramirez is known for, but they nonetheless convey conspicuous leisure. By wearing shorts during the hot, humid Chicago summer, the White Sox suggested that they, unlike other baseball players that endure these conditions, were comfortable and cooler than they might otherwise be—perhaps more so than even the fans in attendance. The Wildcats exuded an air of leisure by incorporating a popular fashion of the time into their on-court appearances, signaling that they were not simply basketball champions, but cool-looking basketball champions, establishing continuity between the players' images on and off the court.

The White Sox and the Wildcats weren't the only athletic teams to incorporate off-the-field luxuries into on-the-field activities; conspicuous leisure is, in fact, quite pervasive. For example, a number of college football teams, whose players must push their bodies to the limit in the sweltering heat of summer, have adapted to wearing shorts during practice sessions. The University of Texas and Auburn University—both in the humid southern United States—wear a variation of football pant bottoms resembling shorts, which have been criticized as bad fashion statements.[12] Yet unlike the game-day attire designed to make an impression, these practice uniforms are simply practical.

These uniforms that push the boundaries of the traditional constitute more than mere fashion failures and short-lived innovations. As items of material culture, these uniforms confound the congruity between audiences' expectations and the image they perceive will accompany them. Indeed, such deviations can confuse audiences, who see athletes as some of the last hardworking figures of the public sphere. Featured in print, over the radio, on television, or on the internet, athletes are still viewed as the gritty, hardworking, and relentless participants of organized competition, and the fans who follow them believe athletes should look the part.

Whether by mandate of management or personal discretion, when these uniforms are altered in a way that suggests conspicuous leisure, the public forum casts judgment. Shorts and collared shirts in baseball, denim in basketball, or any other such alterations fail not because they are somehow inherently bad or impractical, but simply because they confuse the conventions of hard work with leisure.

CHAPTER 3

Betamax

In the fall of 2006, I had just begun my first full-time position as an assistant professor of sociology. Green and straight out of graduate school, I was eager to teach and bursting with interesting information about the world of social dynamics still fresh in my head. I was also poised to impress upon my audience of students that I was at the forefront of technology, with my laptop and jump drive jam-packed with PowerPoint presentations. Unfortunately, some of the material I was presenting had not yet been converted to digital files, still bound to those black cassettes known as Video Home System recordings—or, more commonly, VHS.

On one occasion I introduced some audiovisual material in class. As I put my lecture on hold for a minute to rummage through my backpack for a VHS cassette, the necks of the eighteen- and nineteen-year-old students seemed to stretch around the lectern, behind which I sought refuge. Under crumpled papers, dried pens, and scattered paperclips was the cassette; I latched onto it, raising it up to the class, apologizing for the interruption, and announcing, "I got it . . . sorry about that . . . here it is!" Although the lectern appeared to have all the audiovisual gadgetry to accommodate faculty lectures, to my surprise, there was no videocassette recorder (VCR) to play the cassette! To add insult to injury, I watched one student gaze at the cassette in wonder, quipping, "What is that?" This was only the first of many reminders that some of the technology I was relying upon was simply out of date.

To be fair, the VHS tape I intended to use was at least somewhat more advanced than the then obsolete Betamax—the video-recording format that once rivaled the VHS. Although both products met the same fate in the end, Betamax's candle burned out years before VHS's, during a time when just about the whole world was using one or the other of these two recording technologies. In the "formatting war" between the two, Betamax was the loser.

Putting failure itself aside for a moment, what makes the tale of Betamax's failure so interesting is not its plunge into disuse, but rather the variety of accounts regarding what actually led to its demise. These accounts involve decisions made by Japanese executives at Sony, the length of recording tape, and a bit of gossip about which recording format was "in bed"—so to speak—with the pornography industry. Of course, modern readers might consider recording formats of this type passé to begin with, as during the early twenty-first century, even DVD formats fell by the wayside, giving way to an even more intense formatting war between Blu-ray and HD DVD. Yet beyond explanations associated with the progression of time and the evolution of technology, it is the more colorful hypotheses about what put the final nail in Betamax's coffin that have become rich failure lore. Before I explain Betamax's descent, however, it's best to explain its rise to the top.

In the spring of 1975, Sony introduced Betamax to the world. Although this was not the first video-recording technology introduced to the mass-market consumers, it may have been the first to command mass appeal. Despite the introduction of similar products—including Sony's very own U-matic format—in Europe, North America, and Asia more than a decade earlier, the compact structure, relatively affordable price, and advanced features of the Betamax really drew consumer interest. Perhaps the Betamax was just cooler than other products on the market.

The first Betamax promotional video released in the United States was truly an audiovisual extravaganza for the time: spinning screens, star-speckled nighttime backgrounds, montages of famous television dramas from yesteryear, and colorful silhouettes of people chatting on the go—all in step, of course, to swanky little beats from a 1970s-style disco sound track. Even viewing it today makes my heels kick up, my shoulders shimmy, and my head bob a bit. In retrospect, all the glitter and shine was probably warranted; after all, it was pushing a machine that could record the output from one of the most popular inventions of the twentieth century: the television.

For the marketers of Betamax, the notion that consumers were missing out on all of television's ability to entertain and inform was a major selling point. Using the marketing equivalent of adolescent peer pressure to be part of the latest dance craze or invited to all the hippest parties and coolest concerts, Sony drove home the point that (1) something was taking place, (2) consumers were too busy to be a part of it, and (3) this new recording device had all the right features to allow them to catch up—albeit with an understandable delay. This was not, after all, time travel.

Consumers flocked to the new technology. Within a couple of years of its release, Sony had sold more than one hundred thousand Betamax machines and would enjoy a steady increase in sales well into the mid-1980s. But it was the

Durable and relatively compact in comparison to its rival, VHS, Betamax cassettes failed to gain the necessary popularity to sustain long-term success. ©iStock/alarico

initial success of Betamax that instilled confidence in Sony's top brass. Indeed, with the taste of this success in his mouth, Akio Morita, chairman of Sony, made the bold if not arrogant move of approaching the executives of potential competitors—including Matsushita (Panasonic), JVC, and RCA—in an attempt to garner concessions from them that would help his product corner the market. Morita was intent on convincing these other companies to support his new product by manufacturing VCRs that were compatible with his Betamax cassettes.

Not surprisingly, the other companies turned down Morita's offer and embarked on a mission to develop a competing format. According to one account, "JVC replied that it preferred to develop its own technology. Konosuke Matsushita, in turn, was unhappy that he had not been consulted about the Betamax design. He, too, declined to participate in producing VCRs for the Betamax system."[1]

Morita's plans to expand backfired, giving way to a race between Betamax and VHS to attract consumers and acquire the loyalty needed to put one of the two formats on top of this emerging market.

Notwithstanding the commencement of this early formatting feud, Morita and his Betamax held considerable ground for some time, carrying with them a great deal of satisfied customers. The average consumer seemed to tout Betamax as not only an invention that was here to stay, but also as the superior technology among all others in the same market. Suffice it to say, Betamax had a strong following.

In the beginning, both products were so novel and resembled each other to such a great extent that it was difficult to establish distinguishing qualities between them. As MIT management professor Michael Cusumano notes,

> Just as Sony's Betamax was essentially a miniaturization of the U-Matic but with more advanced recording technique, the VHS closely resembled the U-Matic (and thus, the Betamax), even though the recording format, tap-handling mechanisms, and cassette sizes remained different. Accordingly, it proved difficult for Sony and JVC, and the firms that carried their machines, to differentiate their products through basic features. Hence, neither Beta nor VHS could gain a technological advantage in design or manufacturing that could be sustained long enough to gain a dominant market position.[2]

Nevertheless, not too long after JVC introduced its VHS, indications about how these two formats would ultimately fare began to emerge. In 1978—ironically, with its sales still increasing—Sony's Betamax fell behind VHS in market share. Betamax would remain second to VHS right up to the day it was discontinued at the end of the 1980s.

Marketing experts who have studied the case suggest that both formats had equal potential early on; however, in at least two instances consumers jumped on proverbial bandwagons that helped to establish the major distinctions between the ventures. According Cusumano, the events leading up to the formatting feud may be characterized as follows:

> Its [Betamax] very scale created a window of opportunity lasting a few years, during which firms with comparable engineering and manufacturing capabilities could challenge Sony, the first mover in refining the technology for consumers as well as in making preparations to exploit the mass market. As demand grew at rates out-stripping the supply capabilities of Sony or any one producer, rapid followers who were also technological pioneers stimulated the occurrence of a first bandwagon that affected the formation of alliances for production and distribution. The emergence of demand for

a complementary product—prerecorded tapes (usually movies)—set off a second bandwagon in the 1980s, as retail outlets for tape rental chose to focus on stocking tapes in the format being adopted by a majority of users, even though Sony's original format still enjoyed substantial acceptance.[3]

Although the combination of these factors certainly contributed to the decline of Sony and the success of JVC, less sophisticated explanations also emerged in the years following Betamax's passing.

With little to no information to account for why the sudden success of Betamax transformed into failure, the public allowed its imagination to run wild, establishing its own narratives for this technology's demise. As the introduction of the internet approached, a story about Betamax's defeat was forming, and before long proliferation of the information superhighway launched an anecdotal account of Betamax's final days. This account involved none other than the growing American pastime of filming, watching, and recording pornography.

Before discussing how porn may have figured into the formatting wars, it is important to note that the jury is still out on whether or not the world of audiovisual eroticism actually tipped the scale in favor of VHS. What is certain, however, is that the gossip about the role of pornography in the development of these technologies is definitely sexier than the conclusions most marketing researchers have arrived at.

The argument that pornography played a role in the downfall of Betamax centers on licensing: simply put, Sony did not allow the licensing of its Betamax products for the recording of pornographic material, while VHS did. According to this account, as the recording (and viewing) of pornographic videos skyrocketed, consumers latched onto the one recording technology that supported adult videos—VHS. In this way, it was porn, not the quality of the product it was viewed on, that sealed Betamax's fate.

Now, this sounds interesting enough, and it certainly makes for a believable story: the demand for pornography drove the market for recording technology. Although there were two types of such technology, pornography could only be viewed on one version of it, and this version, VHS, is the one that stood the test of time. Yet this isn't the whole story; in reality the reasons for the failure of Betamax were far less stimulating.

It is unquestionably true that Sony denied licensing for the use of its cassettes to companies that produced pornographic content. It's also true that VHS allowed such licensing, garnering the pornographic market share and perhaps contributing to the increase in viewership of pornography by providing the one format that could support its content. Yet it is difficult to make the claim that the impact of the porn industry alone on video-recording technology was larger than that of all other forms of entertainment combined. Without comparable data on both the content-specific markets as well as the differences in sales between these markets, there's really no way to tell how strong an impact pornography had on these formatting wars.

The pornography factor, however, is not without its pundits—especially in the wake of Betamax's obsolescence. Indeed, as recently as 2008, discussions about the subsequent formatting war between Sony's Blu-ray and HD DVD were rife with implications about whether Sony's continued reluctance to allow licensing of its products for pornography would end up creating the sequel to the company's lack of success with Betamax. According to Ian Rowley of *Bloomberg Businessweek*,

> Legend has it adult entertainment killed Sony's Betamax. Will porn producers' choice of HD-DVD spell trouble for the company's Blu-ray format? . . . Is a sequel in the works? There are some similarities in the current high definition disk format war for supremacy of next-gen DVD players. . . . Explanations for HD-DVD's lead are familiar, too. Producers of adult content complain about higher costs of producing content that syncs with Blu-ray—and that Sony declines to work with adult content vendors.[4]

Rowley and others certainly beat a drum that emphasized the porn factor, but in the end, it was actually the "clean living" of Sony that won the battle this time around. Of course, those who still find merit in the porn factor might chalk up the loss of HD DVD to the introduction of even newer digital formats that allow for unlimited access to pornography using computers and smartphones, rendering recording media irrelevant.

Aside from this rather juicy hypothesis, there were still other explanations for the failure of Betamax that were as believable as they were practical. Indeed, perhaps one of the most probable explanations was its recording length: where VHS cassettes allowed for a three-hour recording time, Betamax allowed for only an hour. As the typical feature-length film runs nearly two hours, one VHS cassette was a much more sensible choice for such films. Sony did eventually catch on to the limitations of Betamax's recording time—even introducing adaptations to increase recording length—but these efforts were simply too late to catch up to VHS. Like its original recording tapes, one could say that Betamax was simply "short on time," as VHS had surpassed it on all accounts.

As it neared the end, Betamax had lost its edge, and an edge of even the smallest proportions was critical to marketability. Yet remarkably, as big contenders in capitalism can't help but breathe every last breath into the fight, Betamax didn't give up. In the waning years before consumers said farewell to Betamax, Sony pushed a final marketing campaign that appeared to sell the good old-fashioned notion of "fun"—a connection that was a bit too tenuous for consumers to draw upon in the era before virtual interaction. A metal box of gears, electrical wiring, and digital displays may be interestingly complex, and the audiovisuals that technology can produce may even be fascinating, but unlike a physical football, baseball, pack of playing cards, Frisbee, and the like, the abstract notion of *fun* was still a hard sell. In a promotional Betamax video from 1987, the narrator consistently attempts to distinguish the Betamax from other VCR devices by stating that Sony's version has "injected fun" into its product.[5] Indeed, the message was quite clear that bedazzling consumers with high-tech bells and whistles should be considered the real attraction, adding: "If you want to re-create the magic of the impressionist masters, digital Betamax offers you three-step mosaic effects, revealing beauty of form and color that will fire your imagination."[6] Yet perhaps the speculation that a little pornography might have livened up Betamax's appeal carried some weight, if not holding the very antidote for preventing its failure by squaring its promise of fun with what consumers had already identified as the next frontier of sex in the coming digital age.

Sony's Betamax went from the highest peaks of success to the lowest valleys of failure—and then underground—in only a matter of decades. It not only commanded a rather respectable market share, it was a trendsetter in new technology. Yet a simple executive decision that smacked of morality in a time when purchasing power was anything but moral—if it ever has been—left enough room to allow Sony's competitors to win the formatting war. Although the short recording length of the tapes may have sealed Betamax's fate, critics and consumers have popularly opted to give credence to the rumor that it was pornography, not recording longevity, that mattered. Perhaps (in a series of perverse double entendres) Betamax's impotence could be chalked up to a lack of experience, stamina, and length—arguably those very virtues that amount to what Sony was trying to sell in Betamax in its final days: *fun.*

CHAPTER 4

LaserDisc

It was 1993 and I was in my last year of junior high school. As mischievous as any fifteen-year-old, I had my share of cutting classes and getting into trouble with my best friend. Although there were plenty of rascally activities for us to get mixed up in, all of them took a backseat to something I think my pal found to be pretty boring: fiddling around with his father's new LaserDisc player. The first time I saw the twelve-inch discs, I was just floored. The packaging was amazing: similar to overgrown compact disc (CD) cases, they opened like books, featured screen shots from the film, and included tons of information that—unlike CD inserts—was printed in a font that could be read without a magnifying glass. The discs themselves were equally impressive; their shiny, metallic appearance was like a cross between my parents' old vinyl records and the flying saucers that were all the rage at the time. Yet above all, due to the quality of the picture, watching films on these discs was as good as, if not better than, watching them in the movie theater.

Despite my raving recollection of LaserDisc, the technology made less of a splash than I would have expected so many years ago. Of the LaserDisc, *Wired* magazine's Matthew Honan quipped: "Predating even the compact disc, the album-sized laser disc was the format of choice for everybody's favorite stoner uncle. His *Star Wars* 'LD' wowed the Walkman set for more than a decade before smaller, all-digital DVDs sent the analog beasts to the curb."[1]

During its thirty-year run between 1978, when it was introduced in North America, and 2009, when Pioneer, the last company to manufacture LaserDisc players, called it quits, the product was more of a model standard that served to inspire the more compact, cheaper, and mass-marketable products that would eventually replace it. Like an older prototypical sibling that encompassed all the qualities and virtues of ideal recording and playback technology, LaserDisc stirred the pot of ingenuity of CDs and mini-disc inventions before ultimately being replaced by digital video discs (DVDs) and Blu-ray.[2]

Under one of its early manufacturing outlets, Magnavox's Magnavision, LaserDisc was showcased as the "next big thing" in home entertainment in a promotional infomercial that featured a fifty-year-old Leonard Nimoy—in an all-white getup with an early 1980s mustache—talking to a blinking and beeping rock. In full futuristic character, Nimoy translates the rock's blinks and beeps, which sing the praises of the new technology and plug its advantages with regard to durability over VHS and Betamax, the major leaders in home entertainment technology of the day. So, as a novel, attractive product that guaranteed superior quality and durability over its competitors—and with commercial representation from a popular space-age celebrity—how is it that LaserDisc found itself situated on the margins of advanced technology, only to be replaced by what seemed like newer versions of itself? Writing in the *New York Times*, Dave Kehr sums up part of the problem: "Laserdiscs emerged as the preferred medium of collectors, offering a sharper image and digital sound, as well as multiple audio tracks that could contain alternate language versions or filmmakers' commentaries. But the double-sided 12-inch discs were bulky and expensive, and relatively few titles were remastered from VHS to take advantage of the laserdisc's technical superiority."[3]

In the end, at least four factors provide some insight to why the LaserDisc failed: (1) outrageous price, (2) lack of rental availability, (3) labor-intensive functionality, and (4) lack of longevity.

LaserDisc technology influenced a number of optical data storage mediums, yet it failed to outlast the very technology it inspired. *Pioneer/ Photofest © Pioneer*

In the early development of LaserDisc, manufacturing, marketing, and sales of the new technology were as exciting as they were costly—particularly in the case of the discs themselves. But this was not initially the case, as one technology blogger notes:

> Discs were originally easier and cheaper to make but the VHS industry spent a lot of time and effort in improving their process. Soon, tapes that started out being expensive to make were being made for less than $1 per unit. In addition, a lot of money went into creating cheaper and better VHS players that more and more consumers could afford. The companies behind the Laserdisc, on the other hand, didn't make as significant investments into their technology and the price per unit never really shrank. Within just a few years, the Laserdisc market saw VHS sales far exceed their own.[4]

Both the players and the discs were expensive to produce and ship, and a good portion of this expense was passed onto the consumers, making it out of reach for the average household budget. The players initially ranged from $500 to $700 apiece, the equivalent of about $1500 to $2500 in today's prices. The discs were also pricey, ranging from $30 to $50 apiece, or nearly $100 in today's prices. In contrast, VHS players sold for between one- and two-thirds the cost of a LaserDisc system, and the tapes were half the price of their flashy competitors. In short, the high cost of the LaserDisc drove the popularity of alternative players, formats, and related technologies.

Unlike the VHS and Betamax rental revolution that gave birth to video stores like Blockbuster, few venues rented LaserDiscs. As Dennis Hunt of the *Los Angeles Times* notes,

> Laser is a buyer's market, dominated by film buffs and affluent fans who are into collecting movies, not renting them. According to David Del Grosso, marketing vice president for the distribution firm Image Entertainment, sales dwarf rentals by a 9–1 ratio. . . . Some people do want to rent, of course, but not enough to make it profitable for most dealers. A retailer who buys a laser disc (about $20–$25 wholesale) for the purpose of renting it (at $2–$4 per day) would need at least 5 to 10 customers to get his money back. With the universe of laser-disc households still very small—about 500,000 nationwide, according to Del Grosso—the odds of that happening on anything but the hottest titles are slim.[5]

In other words, if you wanted to watch a movie on LaserDisc, you were pretty much committed to purchasing it.

LaserDisc also had a quirky function that required owners to intervene and manually operate a part of the viewing experience: every half hour, owners had to eject the disc and flip it over, as the early discs held only thirty minutes of data. Although advances in technology eventually remedied this inconvenience, from what I viewed in the online commentary about LaserDisc's demise, the blemish remained, and many consumers assumed that they would still have to participate in some of the system's functions.

Expensive systems, rental inavailability, and manual interventions in support of the LaserDisc's functions were compounded by a bit of a broken guarantee about the durability of the discs. Where the cheaper and increasingly popular videocassettes sometimes suffered tape entanglement, tears, creases, and contact-related deterioration, the LaserDiscs were supposedly ultraresilient, as they had only a laser to contend with. Nevertheless, the discs suffered from "laser-rot," a problem associated with the adhesives that solidify the bond between the two sides of the disc that gradually degraded the discs' audio and video quality.

By the time LaserDisc was phased out, a confluence of DVD, Blu-ray, and downloadable or streaming online viewing had already taken hold as the preferred mediums to viewing movies. When viewers established this preference over LaserDisc by adopting viewing habits in connection to at least some of these new mediums, the once superior quality of LaserDisc's audio and video was not only overlooked, but just about forgotten.

CHAPTER 5

The Mullet

Hair, a filament of dead protein cells, has had a significant role in countless social institutions throughout history. The intentions surrounding everything from its presence and absence to its texture, length, and color have served as religious, political, social, cultural, and even countercultural features for a variety of social movements, and the fashion in which it is styled has resonated across popular culture through perceptions of hairdos and hairdon'ts. One hairstyle that has received its fair share of publicity—good and bad—in the past thirty years is the mullet, a hairstyle that is generally short up front, cropped low on the sides, and left long in the back. Also known as the "ape-drape," the "bi-level," the "lobster," "mud-flaps," "schlong," and the "sho-lo" (short in the front and long in the back), the mullet, since its heyday in the 1980s, has acquired a certain stigma as a style that has lost its popularity, and, with the exception of the few brave and bold souls who have hung on to it, it has largely fallen into disuse.

In the early stages of my work on this book, for example, I looked for volunteers to model various fashion failures so I could photograph them for use as visuals. I was particularly keen to get images of the mullet, yet due to the length of time it takes to grow one's hair out, the imposition it might pose to have one's hair styled in that way, and even the mere thought of oneself displayed for eternity in a book on failure (sporting a mullet, no less) made my search for a model difficult at best. Fortunately, I had a close friend (whom I will call Greg) who was willing to assist me in my research: perhaps less fortunately for him, he was fashion-trapped in the mid-1980s and had modeled a perfect mullet on a daily basis for more than two and a half decades. Nearly every friend or acquaintance I approached suggested I ask Greg for his permission, as it was apparent that his hairstyle fit the bill.

Yet when the moment arrived, it could not have been more uncomfortable. With dinner and several drinks behind us, I turned to Greg and said, "When

In addition to releasing his 2006 song, "I Want My Mullet Back," Billy Ray Cyrus sported the mullet hairdo for several years during the early 1990s. © *Photofest*

you gonna let me photograph that mullet of yours for my book?" It was as if the record had stopped abruptly and silence befell the restaurant. Greg looked up, zeroed in on my eyes, and said, "Mullet? What mullet?" And he meant it! After I explained what I meant, he seemed bewildered and even offended; he genuinely did not believe his hairdo was this mullet I was referring to, nor did he think it could be perceived as being "out of style." It was one of the most awkward moments of our friendship, but it was also at that moment that I realized some individuals are simply not aware of the nomenclature associated with certain fashions, and they often don't consider their hairstyles to be subject to some qualitative perception of what's "in" versus what's "out."

With this moment of reflexivity suspended in mind, this chapter is the first in this book that grapples with the subjectivity associated with style. Given the enormous variation between and among styles, it appears futile to attempt to categorize styles into popular and unpopular.[1] So the mullet is adjudicated herein through my exploration of popular culture and anecdotal observations that have been published in various places—and certainly not through definitive scientific research.

This exploration of popular culture combined with the gathering of anecdotal observations can lead to some rather telling insights. Take, for example, the following individual's account of her botched attempt at having her hair styled, due in part to the stigma perceived to be associated with the mullet she eventually received:

> So, I sought "The Rachel" [a hairstyle modeled after the role of "Rachel" from the popular sitcom *Friends*] at the bargain haircut chain where I was served by a monster named Jo-ette. Jo-ette smoked compulsively for the duration of our hair-cutting session. The scissors wielded by her nicotine-stained fingers encountered a flowing mass of long locks acquired while attending a retired hippie commune, and wreaked stylistic havoc. I walked out that day with a coif much more resembling another, far less prestigious mane trend—that of the mullet. I wanted to be the girl that guys looked at because something about her reminded them of that really hot girl on *Friends*. Instead, I was that girl that guys looked at because something about her re- minded them of their cousin Billy-Bob from the sticks.[2]

This comment—combining popular culture with anecdotes from social encounters—illuminates some dynamics of the hairstyle, the people who cut and style it, those who sport it, and the feelings associated with it. On the sur- face, the mullet may be a hairstyle, yet why it is considered a "bad hairstyle" is the focus of this chapter.

To begin, the mullet as a social phenomenon is anything but simplistic. In fact, some academics in the social sciences have found the complexities of this haircut worthy of research. As the comment above about the "Rachel" fiasco illustrates, it is the mullet that somehow conjures up a nexus of signification. In their article "Sho-Lo Showdown," Jodi Schorb and Tania Hammidi demon- strate that the mullet—as a feature of lesbian communities—is actually a highly complex hairstyle that embodies meaning negotiated well beyond its mere ap- pearance. Noting that their research revealed a "hair meritocracy," Schorb and Hammidi consider the multitude of perceptions revolving around the mullet as exemplars of just how complicated wearing it can be:

> The sho-lo attains regional signification (as rural, country, or southern—and its derogatory counterparts, hick and redneck), class markings (working class or lower class), racial markings (white but, more specifically, white trash or white racist), and male affiliations (butch, tough butch). As such the sho-lo is associated with aspects of lesbian communities many do not want to preserve: a lack of style (equated with a lack of power), a lack of class status (also linked to power), an over-identification with male power (equated with a rejection of the feminine), a rejection of the rural (favoring a tendency towards perceived urbanity), and a conflation of the rural with bigotry.[3]

These observations may suggest that the mullet is much less a *hairstyle* and much more a *lifestyle*; that is, the significance of the mullet, as something that generates negative perceptions, seems to act as an unsubstantiated indicator of one's shortcomings to those who may not know much about what the style actually means to the individual who wears it.

What seems to be at the forefront of this type of fashion determinism is what styles appeal to the public's sense of beauty. In other words, what is viewed as popular, whether apparent or stereotypic, is often aligned with similar public perception. In their study of beauty, Tania Hammidi and Susan Kaiser note that what individuals consider beautiful is actually contingent upon a process of "visually articulating and negotiating cultural contradictions and personal ambivalences (i.e., conflicting emotions)."[4] Although it may go without saying, it is useful to establish that beauty is, as Hammidi and Kaiser confirm, a social construct, not a natural or inherent feature of human beings.

With this emphasis placed on popular, stylish, or even the successful status of appearances, it is also important to establish that inclusion is not necessarily an indication, determinant, or characteristic of such status. Building upon the theoretical work of Patricia and Peter Adler that focuses on the dynamics of exclusion,[5] David Locher argues in his research on failures of subcultures that

> [s]ubcultures (punk, gothic, metal, etc.) are frequently exclusive; the members accept others into the group not based entirely on what the individual likes (as an inclusive subculture would), but on what he or she does *not* like. . . . The issue involved in such arguments points to the exclusive nature of the subcultures: it is not enough to like that which the other members like, one must also dislike that which the other members do not like.[6]

Indeed, Schorb and Hammidi confirm this very line of reasoning in relation to the mullet hairstyle and its use among lesbian communities. Schorb and Hammidi note from their insider perspective that, "as in most communal identity-formation projects, lesbians tend to define ourselves as much by what we are, as what we are *not*."[7] Thus, exclusion of a particular style or fashion and what it may represent to the general public embodies a defining feature that serves to solidify the bonds among individuals. In this instance, the mullet and its accompanying stigma may actually generate group dynamics that allow for its acceptance or rejection.

So where did the stigma accompanying the mullet originate? One point of departure may be the mullet's senescence among celebrities—those individuals who arguably popularize just about everything from hairstyles and clothing to facial expressions and the other nuances of bodily gesture. Indeed, celebrities such as David Bowie, George Clooney, Jane Fonda, David Hasselhoff, Florence

Henderson, and Mel Gibson—to name just a few—have all sported the mullet at one time, yet one would be hard-pressed to find their current hairstyles bearing any resemblance to those of their earlier years. In this way, the mullet has acquired a stigma not necessarily for its appearance, but instead because it is démodé.

The decline in popularity of this hairstyle, however, may also have something to do with the way it has been publicly lampooned in the popular media. Literature, music, film, and television have all contributed their share of mullet defamation. Among the more popular literature pieces, in 1999 Mark Larson and Barney Hoskyns published *The Mullet: Hairstyle of the Gods*, a charming book that cleverly explores the world of mullets and ultimately gives every indication that the hairstyle is in decline. Larson's book was followed in 2007 by Alan Henderson's *Mullet Madness! The Haircut That's Business up Front and a Party in the Back*, an equally charming piece of literature featuring photographs of some of the most outrageous mullets in history and humorously intimating that the hairstyle has met its demise.

In music, the Beastie Boys demarcated "the end" of the mullet in 1994 when they released "Mullet Head" on their album *Ill Communication*. The track captures characteristics of the mullet and eternally positions them in time, referencing bits of pop culture and styles from the 1980s that have lost their popularity.[8] The punk band the Vandals also offered a musical statement on the hairstyle, referring to the mullet as an "ape drape."[9]

Although the Beastie Boys and the Vandals used parody in their lyrics, others have made more sincere gestures toward the mullet and its significance in their own lives. In 2006 country music singer Billy Ray Cyrus—once an icon of the mullet-wearing tradition—released the song "I Want My Mullet Back,"[10] a twangy tune nostalgically lamenting the loss of youth, his 8-track, his Camaro, and, of course, his mullet.

In 2001, Party in the Back Productions released *American Mullet*, a documentary directed by Jennifer Arnold surveying the hairstyle's wearers and critics along with others whose lives have been affected by encounters with it. In that same year Columbia Pictures released the film *Joe Dirt*, a reasonably well-received comedy featuring a mullet-wearing David Spade. The talented Spade delivered a ninety-one-minute performance that pulled no punches in acting out just about every hillbilly stereotype imaginable. If the mullet were not yet associated with the shortcomings of people on the edge of having nothing—including education, class, and style—*Joe Dirt* made that connection.

Perhaps the real denouement for the mullet came in 2003 when the television network UPN aired *The Mullets*, a sitcom produced by Bill Oakley and Josh Weinstein that featured Dwayne and Denny Mullet, brothers who sported hairstyles they characterized as "business in the front, party in the back." Pushing

Joe Dirt (2001), directed by Dennie Gordon and starring David Spade, brought the mullet out of the 1980s and into the twenty-first century. *Columbia Pictures/ Photofest © Columbia Pictures*

the redneck and hillbilly stereotypes to the max, the Mullet brothers' performance capitalized on the clashes between the realities of popular fashion with the backward styles of pop cultural lag and backwater parlance. Running only one season before it was canceled due to poor ratings in 2004, *The Mullets* was a glaring indication that not even a television show that parodied such a poor fashion statement could be a success.

Popular efforts to make a bad hairdo look even worse did not stop there. On the internet, for example, there is no shortage of quirky websites that showcase the mullet. MulletJunky.com—a website that encourages viewers to "mull it over"—colorfully displays photographs of mullets, complete with humorous instructions for becoming a "mullet hunter" (one who stealthy captures mullet imagery in action); techniques for "hunting mullets" (a guide for adhering to mullet-hunting conventions); and a host of colloquial mullet adaptations, including the "Femullet" (females sporting the hairstyle), "Mullatinos" (Latinos who don the hairdo), and the "Scullet," "Bullet," and "Forcecullet" (variations of scull-bearing, balding, and forced-into-mulletacy mullets).

Another website, RateMyMullet.com, allows individuals to post a photograph of a mullet and put it to the test of popular democracy. As stated on its website:

> RateMyMullet.com is a place where mullet lovers and haters alike
> can join forces and take an active part in voting and commenting
> on the world's best and worst mullets. As you can see, we divide our
> mullets into two sections. The first being "Senior Mullets," which are
> mullets over the age of 18. The second category is "Junior Mullets"
> which contains some of the world's top up and coming mullets.[11]

As pervasive as the internet can be, it is no wonder that the mullet has found no quarter in popular culture.

But aside from these and other factors, something could be said about the physical dimensions of the mullet that contribute to its poor appearance. Could the mullet's downfall have something to do with its disproportionate dimensions? That is, could having less hair in the front, top, and sides of one's head in proportion to what extends from the back of it cause a sense of symbolic disorder to the perception of fashion aficionados? In her 1966 treatise on the origins of perceptions toward dirt and difference, Mary Douglas goes to great lengths to argue that what is considered dirty, dangerous, and not worthy of regard is *not* based upon some universal concept of health, sanitation, or even habit, but instead that such aberrations from the norm seem to disrupt some imagined symbolic order. In this way, and in contrast to some cultural critics, such binaries between good and bad, fashionable and unfashionable, or success and failure may be based not upon arbitrary notions of what constitutes a universal right or wrong way to appear, but instead the rules and regulations that come to fore in determining this are actually part of a larger system of symbolic boundary maintenance. As Douglas argues,

> Granted that disorder spoils pattern; it also provides the materials
> of pattern. Order implies restriction; from all possible materials, a
> limited selection has been made and from all possible relations a
> limited set has been used. So disorder by implication is unlimited,
> no pattern has been realized in it, but its potential for patterning
> is infinite. This is why, though we seek to create order, we do not
> simply condemn disorder. We recognize that it is destructive to
> existing patterns; also that it has potentiality. It symbolizes both
> power and danger.[12]

Although abstract, this argument would suggest that the construction of order, even when materialized through fashion, is merely part of a larger economy of symbols that generate boundaries—that which extends away from what is often viewed as conditionally pure, safe, secure, and by extension, stylish.

In the end, the stigma attached to the mullet and its image as unpopular cannot be attributed to any one cause, but instead a host of factors in combination have led to its fashionable decline. Although the mullet may be categorized as part of bad fashion in general and a bad hairstyle in particular, it is important to remember that it did, in fact, once have a heyday. Ultimately, however, the "short up front and long in back" look does not appear to have much of a future.

CHAPTER 6

BluBlocker Sunglasses

Throughout the twentieth and twenty-first centuries, celebrities have influenced the fashion world by their appearance both within and beyond the spotlight. It may have been James Dean who inspired the fashions of the lively rebels and outcasts from the late 1950s with his iconic combination of white T-shirts and blue jeans. The personal trials of Johnny Cash were suppressed through his public reinvention after appearing everywhere in all black. In a period of much-needed change surrounding civil rights, young Angela Davis's Afro-styled coif, accompanied by her fist firmly held high, demarcated a look that showcased a cultural power movement. And when the Beatles toured India, the band that had made peace and understanding their modus operandi appropriated the colorful pajama style of their surroundings and watched it reverberate through their fan following and beyond.

Although these styles may not necessarily emerge sui generis from those who initially popularize them, viewing our own image in light of what appears in mass circulation can reaffirm just how much we depend on the looks of others. As many of the styles Americans give life to each day are subtly informed by the images we are routinely bombarded with, the world of celebrity styles is a useful starting point for determining what works and what does not in the world of fashion.

Somewhere between the hairstyle and the wardrobe that is tied, buttoned, cinched, or draped over our body is the pair of sunglasses that rest on the bridge of our nose—the one convenient, though never really necessary, item of material culture that seems to establish one's sense of style pro forma. Perhaps worn during the day for protection or in the evening to disguise one's indiscretions, most sunglasses carry with them a statement.

When commercially marketed, sunglasses and the brands they bear reach out to onlookers and symbolically express something about the individuals who wear them.[1] Some sunglasses, like the Ray Ban Jackie OHH II, designed after the pair worn by the late Jacqueline Kennedy Onassis, are intentionally manufactured as personality links, giving the impression that the bearer of this style is somehow connected to the legacy of the person who once wore them. Others, like Ivana Trump's sunglass lines, have been marketed intentionally by the current bearers of these products themselves.

Still others, like the focus of this chapter, may have something of a facetious relationship with the world of sunglasses and the individuals who wear them. The brand is BluBlockers, and the tongue-in-cheek reference is to the company's humble beginnings. Rather than hiring a celebrity such as Brad Pitt, Eva Longoria, George Clooney, or Beyoncé—or their equivalent for the time—the young company enlisted the talents of a lesser known figure. On the sunny beaches of Los Angeles, California, a hitherto unknown artist named Dr. Geek used his bouncy rap to launch the BluBlocker line. If the dragging thud of a beatbox rhythm has started to thump in your head and you can see in your mind a young man in a black sombrero, you were probably exposed to one of the more joked-about—albeit successful—marketing ventures of the late 1980s. A truncated video of the decades-old infomercial starring Dr. Geek has gone viral in the virtual world—a playful reminder that the marketing of products can carry just as much comic capital as the products that eventually become passé themselves.

BluBlocker sunglasses became famous because of Dr. Geek and his minute-and-a-half rap. Though certainly not as lively as Dr. Geek's performance, the sunglasses themselves were moderately large-rimmed aviator-style sunglasses that were said to do more than just guard against the sun, stopping 100 percent of blue light—a high-energy visible light that is harmful to our health in a number of ways. The creation of BluBlockers was a brilliant example of innovation and the company should be commended for its vision.

According to its website, not even the sky was the limit for BluBlocker Corporation; the product began with a project that sought solutions to problems with visibility in outer space:

> The origins of BluBlocker® Sunglasses started with the NASA space program. Astronauts needed strong protection for their eyes in outer space where ultraviolet rays were much stronger than on earth.
>
> A California sunglass manufacturer designed a pair that not only blocked UV rays but blue rays as well. By blocking blue rays, objects would appear sharper and clearer since blue light did not focus on the retina which is the focusing screen of your eye.
>
> The astronauts eye protection didn't get much publicity until a Chicago entrepreneur, Joseph Sugarman[,] was driving as a passenger in a car driven by the sales representative for the NASA sunglasses. The sales representative noticed Sugarman was squinting and offered

him a pair of NASA sunglasses. Sugarman noticed how clear things appeared and how it stopped him from squinting.[2]

As it turns out, BluBlocker was at the cutting edge of something quite advanced. Indeed, as researchers are now confirming, exposure to blue light may reduce melatonin secretion, particularly when that exposure comes in the form of artificial lighting from household electronics that remain powered on. This reduction in melatonin can affect the regularity and sufficiency of an individual's sleeping patterns. Although it does not specifically endorse BluBlockers, the *Harvard Health Letter* all but directly advised that such glasses can minimize exposure to blue light.[3]

So how did the marketing magic surrounding this advanced technology become such a fashion failure? The simple answer is that it did not. BluBlocker Corporation is doing just fine. But is the company's commercial success based upon a conscious decision by consumers to protect their vision and sport a swanky style, or do individuals who purchase BluBlockers hold those qualities secondary to seeking a look that conjures up nostalgia for the meretricious style of the late 1980s?

If celebrity style is any indication of the seriousness with which consumers imitate, the popularity of the look does not appear to have been so pervasive. In actuality, only a few popular figures publicly strapped on these sunglasses. Former Chicago Bears star quarterback Jim McMahon not only wore BlueBlockers, he also promoted them for a time.[4] And in the popular 2001 film *The Royal Tenenbaums*, Richie Tenenbaum, played by Luke Wilson, appears to sport the sunglasses throughout the movie. A young tennis star turned suicidal adult, Wilson's character rarely removed his sunglasses. His dim pastiche of retro chic threads—including a moisture-wicking tennis outfit, loosely shrouded in a khaki-colored two-piece suit and topped with a red, white, and blue striped headband—was accompanied by sunglasses that look like BluBlockers. But although the internet has branded them as such, Wilson's shades are said to be the Vuarnet PX-3000 Aviators[5]—close enough, at least in terms of image recognition!

In 2009, BluBlockers were featured in the film *The Hangover*.[6] In his role as the eccentric brother-in-law-to-be, Zach Galifianakis entertained audiences with his quirky one-liners, erratic behavior, and strange getups. Galifianakis appears several times sporting his BluBlockers—at times, accompanied by not much else. But similar to Wilson's role in *The Royal Tenenbaums*, Galifianakis's character in *The Hangover* is rather strange. This was not exactly the type of publicity a young Tom Cruise gave to Ray Ban in 1983 when he wore a pair in *Risky Business*, or Daniel Craig delivered to Tom Ford in 2008 when he sported those shades as 007 in *Quantum of Solace*. Indeed, no BluBlocker-wearing celebrity ever really launched the sunglasses onto the world stage of famous cultural artifacts.

The 2009 hit *The Hangover* featured Zach Galifianakis as the eccentric and wildly popular character Alan, sporting demi tortoise nylon BluBlocker sunglasses. *Warner Bros./ Photofest © Warner Bros.*

But in contrast to all the jabs BluBlockers have taken, the company has had relatively good success with its fashion accessories. BluBlockers are still making headway in the industry and have even been recognized as somewhat popular items. In 2012, BluBlocker Corporation was invited to attend the Latin Grammy Awards in Las Vegas in no small way: the glasses were included in the coveted artist and celebrity appreciation gift bags.[7] Given this degree of success, it may be more appropriate to speak of BluBlockers as a rarity in material culture: the non-failure failure.

If we think of failure metaphorically as any of a number of obstacles along the unpredictable road to success, we can subtly separate these obstacles of failure from the item's successes. Thus, it follows that the BluBlocker Corporation is not a failure, but instead has been the focus of some poor publicity—the kind of publicity that Americans connect with precisely because it conjures up a sense of something failure-esque. (Similar non-failure failures in recent memory include, for example, the Shamwow, the Snuggie, the Chia Pet, the Clapper, the Tae Bo workout system, and even the $29.95 Earl Scheib paint job.)

As with other products made popular mostly by television infomercials, the parody of the BluBlocker sunglasses has little to do with the quality of the glasses themselves. Instead, most of the banter directed toward BluBlockers emerged as a result of the infomercial that spawned its initial popularity. The infomercial, released in 1987, features a seemingly impromptu sales pitch to a group of attentive onlookers in Venice Beach, California, given by a young hip-hop artist known as Dr. Geek. A real attention-getter, Dr. Geek was a heavyset man wearing a T-shirt featuring Curly from *The Three Stooges*, a wide-brimmed sombrero, and a pair of aviator BluBlockers, cheerfully embracing an oversized beige boom box blaring the beats of his now infamous jam. The ridiculousness of the scene—now readily available on several video sharing websites—may have been the real hook of the infomercial, making it one of the more humorous selections of 1980s lore.

In 2010 *Time* magazine listed the infomercial as number fourteen on its list of the twenty-five worst infomercials. Parodying Dr. Geek's delivery, journalist Chris Gentilviso conjured up some of the same beats the original commercial delivered more than twenty years ago:

> His name is Geek, and he's more than a hip-hopper. He prides himself as a savvy sunglasses shopper. Thousands of pairs of Blu-Blocker sunglasses have been sold with a little help from this Venice Beach, Calif., rapper and his *guapo* sombrero. . . . The glasses sell as a "safe and effective way to prevent eye damage." Ear damage? Not so much.[8]

Bad advertising or not, the humor involved truly created a marketing success, yet the company has never really shaken the tomfoolery that distinguished it from other commercial products from its overall image. Those who remember the BluBlocker infomercial still get a little chuckle out of it—even if they are on their way to purchase the shades for themselves.

Categorizing BluBlockers as either a success or a failure is complicated. On the one hand, they have stood the test of time (more than two decades), the company has developed its product line to accommodate a variety of occasions, and the sunglasses have been honored by their inclusion in the swag bags for one of the fastest growing music award ceremonies in the country—all rather impressive indications that the sunglasses company is a success. But its history is colored by the corny imagery of the past that fails to reflect this success. Indeed, BluBlocker's humble beginnings—and in particular its association with the 1987 infomercial—are conjoined with the regally bad fashion that flourished in the 1980s. BluBlockers are the sophisticated close pop-cultural cousins of such items as the foam-mesh combination trucker hat, the rainbow-striped knee-high athletic socks, the rubber flip-flops, and even design-lined, crimped, or mullet hairdos! BluBlockers are the interestingly good part of a bad thing. They constitute the salvageable leftovers of more than twenty kitsch-filled years of failed products and productions. They survive as clever props adorning the faces of some celebrities in movies (even if only mistaken as such), remarketed through the creative appropriation of the original 1987 infomercial recirculating through internet mashups, and, of course, the company's reinvention of itself with an expanding product line that anyone can find alive and well on the BluBlocker website.

CHAPTER 7

Zubaz

It may go without saying, but it is a fact that fashions come and go. One fashion known as "leg paint" came and went due to the mandates of wartime necessity. During World War II, nylons were rationed by the United States military, who needed the material to use in manufacturing everything from parachutes to shoelaces. Almost immediately, women's love for nylon hosiery became something less than a bare necessity, forcing women to either bare their legs or paint them on. A common practice among women longing for the crisscross patterns of fishnets or the sleek darning line running up their legs was to test their steady hands at drawing them on. For a much more uniform look, the Armand Company marked a product known as Stocking Stick, which was paint that would slightly tan wearers' legs to imitate the look of nylons. But nylons returned to store shelves shortly after the war, marking the end of the leg paint fad.

Decades later, in January 1990, the world of rap and fashion were hit with a double whammy when MC Hammer released his hit album *Please Hammer, Don't Hurt 'Em*. On the album was Hammer's most popular song, "U Can't Touch This," which featured a catchy riff sampled from Rick James's popular hit "Super Freak." But in the place of James's sparkly early 1980s funk fashion of long, braided hair and tight-fitting pants, Hammer introduced a look featuring pastels, tightly tapered hairdo, and baggy trousers. As Hammer shuffled across the studio in unison with his backup dancers, the choreography seemed to take a backseat to the fluttering motion of their pants, as the fabric mirrored their every move. Like flags gyrating in the wind, the excess textile suggested a bold, if not larger-than-life, image for the pants' physical and symbolic presence. This was unquestionably part of Hammer's intention, as the pants—like the fame he had recently acquired—were exactly what the chorus of his song explicitly reminded audiences of: that which you, the commoner, could not touch.

Rapper MC Hammer in his signature Hammer pants. © *Photofest*

The exclusivity of the pants did not last long, however, as retailers came running to supply the demand. Hammer's pants soon caught the attention of fans and fashionistas alike, some referring to them as "parachute pants," "drop-crotchers," or "Turkish trousers," while still others simply dubbed them "Hammer pants." There were also those that saw this look as a clear throwback to the zoot suit popularized in the 1940s. But the look was actually the cultural appropriation of an Indian style known as "harem pants"—a baggy pair of trousers with multiple pleats and tapered at the ankles.

Origins aside, to American audiences the look was new, and soon it was springing up everywhere. Not only did celebrities jump on the bandwagon, but even those who chose to make their own clothes were accommodated when the pattern company Simplicity released the "MC Hammer Pants" pattern. Yes, it seemed that everyone, regardless of socioeconomic status, could slip into the voluminous clothing worn by Hammer himself.

At roughly the same time—but perhaps owing to totally unrelated circumstances—another baggy-pant phenomenon was emerging out of Minnesota. In 1989, Joseph Michael Laurinaitis and Michael Hegstrand—two professional wrestlers of the choreographed entertainment kind—introduced a roomy style of pants that targeted weightlifters, affording these potential customers a better range of motion, lessening the constraints of typical workout outfits. Laurinaitus and Hegstrand (also known as Road Warrior Animal and Road Warrior Hawk, respectively) pitched the concept to Bob Truax and Dan Stock, who later ran with the idea and marketed the pants as Zubaz.

Zubaz were, at the very least, an interesting spectacle. Like the Hammer pants, their crotch was set low, with baggy outer thighs and tapered ankles. Just like Hammer's style? Well, not quite. Unlike Hammer pants, which were mostly one solid color, Zubaz originally featured a zebra pattern of alternating black and white stripes—and soon enough the patterns and color configurations ran were almost endless. Indeed, Zubaz began mixing and matching colors and team logos for the Tampa Bay Storm and the New Orleans Night of the new Arena Football League, soon followed by styles and patterns for just about every major sporting team. If professionals were playing a game that fans were watching, the teams' colors and their logos could be "Zubazed."

With MC Hammer sporting his signature trousers in more wildly popular music videos, Truax and Stock pushing the threads to market, and the Road Warriors sporting the new style on the World Championship Wrestling circuit, the look had taken hold. Yet it wasn't long before the fanfare settled and the pants transformed from something that one *couldn't* touch to something that one *wouldn't* touch.

Even those fashions that go belly up are interesting items of material culture to social scientists. In an article published at the turn of the twentieth century, German sociologist Georg Simmel makes the case for the social significance of fashion. In his piece, Simmel argues that fashion is both a form of "imitation" and "social equalization"—the former an action endowed with a desire to be like the elite, and the latter an attempt by the nonelite to dissolve difference and distinction.[1] As he notes, "[T]wo social tendencies are essential to the establishment of fashion, namely, the need of union on the one hand and the need of isolation on the other. Should one of these be absent, fashion will not be formed—its sway will abruptly end."[2] For Simmel, the fact that fashions change so rapidly is an empirical example of classes trying to assert control by either establishing and maintaining distinction or abolishing it altogether. As Simmel writes,

Fashion is the imitation of a given example and satisfies the demand for social adaptation; it leads the individual upon the road which all travel, it furnishes a general condition, which resolves the conduct of every individual into a mere example. At the same time it satisfies in no less degree the need of differentiation, the tendency towards dissimilarity, the desire for change and contrast, on the one hand by a constant change of contents, which gives to the fashion of today an individual stamp as opposed to that of yesterday and of tomorrow, on the other hand because fashions differ for different classes—the fashions of the upper stratum of society are never identical with those of the lower; in fact, they are abandoned by the former as soon as the latter prepares to appropriate them. Thus fashion represents nothing more than one of the many forms of life by the aid of which we seek to combine in uniform spheres of activity the tendency towards social equalization with the desire for individual differentiation and change.[3]

As Simmel's work suggests, this notion of fashion is complicated by class structures, but—and perhaps even more important—fashion is inextricably related to how people attempt to create differentiation as well as destroy it.

Of course, Simmel's ideas apply here to the case of the life and death of Zubaz. The rise of this style's popularity is a case study in the imitation of elite fashion. Although it might be a stretch to assume that MC Hammer, a couple of professional wrestlers, and some body-building garment entrepreneurs could be considered the kind of elite Simmel was referring to, in accordance with his discussion of the incessant transformation of fashion, times do in fact change. In this instance, celebrity, performative crazes, and body-building fads were certainly influential substitutes for the affluent of Simmel's era. In fact, I would argue that today's true class-based elite are largely interested in maintaining their privacy far from the spotlight of popular media, while the icons and products of popular culture are a much more influential factor—especially during the early 1990s, when America was at the doorstep of the Information Age.

As the popularity of Zubaz increased, imitation was first and foremost a determining factor of their dissemination. The conformity involved herein lends itself to the comfort individuals experience when they need not think or even do for themselves, instead simply imitating the styles of others. For Simmel, this notion of imitation has a rather alluring element to it:

The charm of imitation in the first place is to be found in the fact that it makes possible an expedient test of power, which, however, requires not great personal and creative application, but is displayed easily and smoothly, because its content is a given quantity. We might define it as the child of thought and thoughtlessness. It affords the pregnant possibility of continually extending the greatest creations of the human spirit, without the aid of the forces which were originally the very condition of their birth. Imitation, furthermore, gives to the individual the satisfaction of not standing alone in his actions. Whenever we imitate, we transfer not only the demand for creative activity, but also the responsibility for the action from ourselves to another. Thus the individual is freed from the worry of choosing and appears simply as a creature of the group, as a vessel of the social contents.[4]

What Simmel might add today, if he were around to witness how fashions come into circulation, is that imitation is not necessarily a bottom-up enterprise. Although fashions may (or may not) originate among the elite, imitation can take place among the lower socioeconomic classes in general. Moreover, the process by which individuals appear to shame others for failing to conform or imitate is germane to Simmel's insight. Indeed, in at least one instance Simmel addresses this very point:

> Inasmuch as we are dealing here not with the importance of a single fact or a single satisfaction, but rather with the play between two contents and their mutual distinction, it becomes evident that the same combination which extreme obedience to fashion acquires can be won also by opposition to it. Whoever consciously avoids following the fashion, does not attain the consequent sensation of individualization through any real individual qualification, but rather through mere negation of the social example. If obedience to fashion consists in imitation of such an example, conscious neglect of fashion represents similar imitation, but under an inverse sign.[5]

In this way, when rejecting a particular fashion and taking an objective stance against it by wearing something unaligned with it, a dissenter is not really maintaining his or her individuality as much as acknowledging the presence of an established fashion. Pushing back against this fashion may appear to be an instance of nonconformity, but only insofar as the dissenter is making concessions to a structural network of how the objective signs embedded within this particular look *could* be imitated but are not. Furthermore, such dissent almost inevitably engenders a new fashion to which the dissenter is now conforming.

Notwithstanding Simmel's analysis, imitation as a hallmark of fashion is not merely a phenomenon of social psychology, but may also be the result of product engineering. During the first half of the twentieth century, the theories and practices associated with the effectiveness of marketing goods were undergoing a paradigmatic overhaul in which enhancing the quality of a given product became secondary to the enterprise of selling it. In other words, to use Marxian terms, the use value of a product, or that multifaceted quality it possessed, was deemphasized and replaced with a suggestion that the product was either passé or on its way to being so. In this way, products were engineered to inconspicuously maximize the profit through their exchange value, and a new model of production was being established to make products that would be considered useless as soon as possible, whether or not they were indeed useless.

The impact of this condition was a bolstering of consumption that had never before been witnessed. Frankfurt School theorist Herbert Marcuse discussed consumption in relation to this form of product engineering in terms of the social constraints it imposed upon individuals. For Marcuse, consumption and the role of production engineering were ominous influences in suppressing human liberation within what he termed the *affluent society*. In a 1967 speech, Marcuse characterizes this societal condition as bound to one's personal ties to commercial goods. As Marcuse notes,

> It [an affluent society] is a society in which . . . material as well as cultural needs of the underlying population are satisfied on a scale larger than ever before—but they are satisfied in line with the requirements and interests of the apparatus and of the powers which control the apparatus. And it is a society growing on the condition of accelerating waste, planned obsolescence and destruction, while the substratum of the population continues to live in poverty and misery.[6]

Of particular significance is Marcuse's mention of *planned obsolescence*: the fundamental concept that products could be made with the intention that they would fail to fulfill expectations, be discarded, contribute to waste, and, in the end, generate a need to buy another product to replace it.

At the forefront of this made-to-fail concept was marketing consultant Victor Lebow. In an article in the *Journal of Retailing*, Lebow outlines a strategy for getting Americans to cash registers as frequently as possible. In one section of his article—under the subheading "The Real Meaning of Consumer Demand"—Lebow writes,

> Our enormously productive economy demands that we make consumption our way of life, that we convert the buying and use of goods into rituals, that we seek our spiritual satisfactions, our ego satisfactions, in consumption. The measure of social status, of social acceptance, of prestige, is now to be found in our consumptive patterns. The very meaning and significance of our lives today is expressed in consumptive terms. The greater the pressures upon the individual to conform to safe and accepted social standards, the more does he tend to express his aspirations and his individuality in terms of what he wears, drives, eats—his home, his car, his pattern of food

serving, his hobbies. These commodities and services must be offered to the consumer with a special urgency. We require not only "forced draft" consumption, but "expensive" consumption as well. We need things consumed, burned up, worn out, replaced, and discarded at an ever increasing pace. We need to have people eat, drink, dress, ride, live, with ever more complicated and, therefore, constantly more expensive consumption. The home power tools and the whole "do-it-yourself" movement are excellent examples of "expensive" consumption.[7]

With consumption as the main priority, Lebow's strategies gave rise to planned obsolescence and perceived obsolescence. The former refers to the manufacturing of products that are created to fail, while the latter refers to a social psychological phenomenon whereby individuals shame each other into making consumption their most important activity. It is this latter form of obsolescence that relates so closely to the failure of Zubaz—fashion, after all, is bound to imitation or lack thereof.

In her animated documentary detailing the negative effects of consumption, Annie Leonard cleverly illustrates just how powerful planned and perceived obsolescences actually are. Focusing on the latter, Leonard briefly mentions a number of items that have been forced into obsolescence, including DVDs, mops, and computers, before arriving at fashions and how their downfall is directly influenced by perceived obsolescence. As Leonard explains,

Have you ever wondered why women's shoe heels go from fat one year to skinny the next, to fat, to skinny? It's not because there's some debate about which heel structure is more healthy for women's feet; it's because wearing fat heels in a skinny heel year shows everybody that you haven't contributed to that arrow [consumption] recently . . . so you're not as valuable as the person in skinny heels next to you, or more likely in some ad—it's to keep us buying new shoes.[8]

The parallels between Leonard's commentary on perceived obsolescence in women's fashion and the failure of Zubaz pants are intriguing. The transition from the slim, form-fitting pants of the 1980s to the baggy look of the 1990s did not take place solely based upon popular culture and consumer demand; it was also influenced by the interconnected activities bound to socialization. To see and be seen is also to take note of others' appearances—and to have one's own appearance be taken note of by others. For producers, marketers, and retailers, all the conditions for manipulating consumption are in place—the only thing missing is good old-fashioned human envy among consumers.

In Simmel's article this notion of envy figures in quite compellingly. According to Simmel,

The fashionable person is regarded with mingled feelings of approval and envy; we envy him as an individual, but approve of him as a member of a set group. . . . There is a shade of envy which includes a species of ideal participation in the envied object itself. An instructive example of this is furnished by the conduct of the poor man who gets a glimpse of the feast of his rich neighbor. The moment we envy an object or a person, we are no longer absolutely excluded from it; some relation or other has been established—between both the same psychic content now exists—although in entirely different categories and forms of sensations.[9]

During the popular rise of Zubaz, envious onlookers—either through curiosity or genuine interest in appropriating the look—found this fashion to be worthy of imitation. In Simmel's terms, acquiring this fashion for one's own was a social endeavor in which individuals latching onto the style were attempting to achieve a sense of equalization by dissolving difference, the simplicity of conforming being only an elementary explanation. However, just as soon as those elite trendsetters got wind of the fact that their style was being taken up by members of the more common classes, fashion underwent another transformation through an equally objective social endeavor in which these trendsetters attempted to maintain the distinction between themselves and the other. In this way, the very failure of Zubaz is, like that of all fashion, subject to the dialectical relationship between the desire of some to establish distinction and the desire of others to remove it.

Like the teeth and their opposing voids within two adjoined cogwheels, the relationship between the forerunners of fashion and the individuals who conform to it are bound to cyclical patterns—patterns for which influence and control are essentially beyond the powers of producers. Indeed, every once in a while a look that has flopped stands back up, brushes itself off, and reappears. As Elizabeth Licata from the *Gloss* notes, once again in recent times "you can wear drop-crotch pants without looking like an asshole."[10] With some variation in cut and style, celebrities like Heidi Klum, Victoria Beckham, Ciara, Leona Lewis, Jennifer Lopez, Jessica Alba, Halle Berry, Justin Bieber, Gwen Stefani, and Rihanna have all rocked the Zubaz style back onto the contemporary public scene.[11]

As recently as 2013, the movie *Pain and Gain*, which showcased the shady side of the body-building subculture, featured the pants in all their hilarity. Staring Mark Wahlberg, Dwayne Johnson, and Anthony Mackie as bodybuilders turned extortionists, the film is riddled with images of Zubaz—images that seem to conjure up a humorous paradox about how hypermasculine men somehow negotiate an indifference to the colors and styles so stereotypically associated with emasculation. These men, with behemoth frames and hyperaggressive attitudes—seem a bit unconvincing in their swirling pastel-colored Zubaz. In one rather graphic scene, Adrian Noel Doorbal (played by Mackie), watching pornography on his television, reaches into his red, yellow, and green Zubaz to masturbate. With ease and convenience Doorbal strokes his erection away, his colorful pants flopping up and down, only to learn that he cannot climax because of his newly revealed impotence.

Even beyond the sphere of popular culture, the dialectics of fashion still surface—sometimes at the very place of origin. Just when one thought Zubaz had seen their last days, they resurfaced in an online marketplace. Complete with a Zubaz photostream where fans can upload favorite pictures of themselves donning the colorful pants, team shops pushing gear for fans, and a whole array of new products that carry at least some pattern or reference to their former look in the gym, the Zubaz website has helped the look to make a modest comeback. "The Pant, the Myth, the Legend"[12] has earned its place in the company of all that once was all the rage when coming onto the scene but is now worn only by those willing to show their age by wearing styles of the past that are rarely seen today.

CHAPTER 8

New Coke

The Coca-Cola Company has been around for more than 130 years, dominating the world soft-drink industry for the vast majority of that time. With only one major competitor—Pepsi—close enough to ever snatch up a considerable portion of the market share, Coca-Cola's only real concern has been staying competitive through innovation. Indeed, Coca-Cola has done just this, offering up a variety of flavors and calorie-conscious configurations like Cherry Coke, Vanilla Coke, Coca-Cola with Lime, Diet Coke, and Coke Zero. In some ways, Coca-Cola has pioneered so much of the terrain that makes up the soft-drink industry that at times it seems that its only real competitor is itself.

In 1985 the Coca-Cola Company actually did something akin to competing with itself by introducing New Coke, a cola intended to be a somewhat sweeter version of the old formula. In terms of packaging, the red aluminum can remained virtually the same, only replacing the graceful white script logo with a silver-colored typeset font and adding a diagonal label that read "NEW!" in black lettering. In this way, some of the external features of the can's appearance broke with Coca-Cola conventions, qualifying it, at least on the surface, as something new—yet the internal features may not have convinced consumers of the value of such novelty.

According to Roberto Goizueta, then CEO of the company, the taste of New Coke was "a matter best left up to poets and copywriters," adding, "I would say it is smoother, uh, uh, rounder yet, uh, yet bolder . . . a more harmonious flavor."[1] Goizueta's abstractions aside, the general marketing pitch was that New Coke was intended to be sweeter than the original. The formula for Coca-Cola had not been substantially altered since 1903, when the company reduced the original amount of coca leaf extract, so the 1985 New Coke formula was a rather significant exception—something thought to be an answer to the encroaching competition of Pepsi, which offered a somewhat sweeter taste.

Upon its release, some consumers and critics were initially impressed. Regarding the product launch itself, Jesse Meyers of *Beverage Digest* remarked, "[T]his has got to be the boldest consumer products move of any kind of any stripe since Eve started to hand out apples."[2] In terms of initial profits, sales told a pretty substantial story: "Many bottlers reported that sales of new Coke were greater than expected and during the first few weeks after the new Coke introduction, the company's weekly survey of 900 respondents showed consumers preferring new Coke over old Coke by a margin of 53% to 47%."[3] Indeed, recorded sales posted an increase of 8 percent in contrast to the same period a year prior.[4]

But despite Coca-Cola's efforts, consumers were not convinced that New Coke was sweeter, better, or even something "new." Reactions ranged from disappointment and satirical disparagement to accusations of deception—and even the emergence of conspiracy theories. Many of the disappointed took to their phones, logging more than a thousand phone calls a day to the 800-GET-COKE hotline.[5] And some of the disappointed took the change far more seriously, as noted by one historian:

> [Some] appeared to be speaking more from their hearts as they likened Coke's switcheroo to a blasphemous assault on their most cherished icons and precepts. Some compared it to burning the flag or rewriting the Constitution. "God and Coca Cola," had been "the only two things in my life," one complained in a letter, "now you have taken one of those things away from me."[6]

The situation was becoming increasingly clear: Coca-Cola fans wanted the original formula, and they were willing to go to what appeared to be some rather ridiculous extremes to get it back.

Soon the disappointed base began to organize, and leading the charge was a fifty-seven-year-old Seattle retiree named Gay Mullins. Applauding Mullins's courage to stand up to a corporation and demand that it earn his and his constituents' business, *People* magazine detailed his fight:

> Gay Mullins had a dream—a wild, wacky, flagrantly unthinkable notion that one man could force a giant corporation to mend its errant ways. Specifically, he dreamed of making Coca-Cola swallow a big loss on its sweeter, supposedly improved "new" Coke and give us back the original. The Real Thing. The true It that Coke is. In that cause Mullins, 57, spent $100,000, almost all of his retirement nest egg.[7]

Mullins truly was instrumental in making the fight to bring back Coca-Cola's original formula a public affair, encouraging his group—Old Cola Drinkers of

Which one is the "Real Thing"? ©iStock/AboutnuyLove

America—to stay focused and organized. Well before the Information Age, Mullins and his group "set up petitions, provided pins with new Coke crossed out, and spoke to the media about their mission."[8]

With Coca-Cola's public affairs in disarray, American's love for humor in the face of failure kicked into full gear. David Letterman cleverly quipped, "Coke's decided to make their formula sweeter, they're going to mix it with Pepsi."[9] Pepsi also took advantage of Coca-Cola's position, launching a commercial that began with a young girl asking, "Somebody out there tell me why Coke did it? Why did Coke change?"[10] In the end, she resolves to try her first Pepsi—and, of course, is gleefully satisfied. Food critic Mimi Sheraton also weighed in on the milieu, writing in a *Time* magazine review, "New Coke seems to retain the essential character of the original version. . . . It tastes a little like classic Coca-Cola that has been diluted by melting ice."[11]

Of course, the long-term fallout was just as comical—perhaps second only to the Edsel—as the characterization of New Coke as a symbol of failure began to spring up all over popular culture: "When an athlete is great, he or she is called the Michael Jordan of his or her sport. When a new product launch is a disaster, it is called the 'New Coke' of its industry."[12]

The most bizarre responses, however, came from fringe commentators claiming that New Coke was actually an inside job designed by Coca-Cola to save money as well as renew its brand's popularity in the face of Pepsi's recent success. Although there are several different versions of the so-called New Coke Conspiracy, the vast majority share a common narrative that goes something like this: Coca-Cola wanted to save money by orchestrating an elaborate plan to replace the sugar in its formula with the much cheaper corn syrup. By touting the intention of sweetening the formula, marketers would build anticipation in consumers of a sweeter concoction, and those consumers might even do some wild psychological acrobatics to convince themselves that New Coke was indeed sweeter. In order to set the wheels rolling on the scam and cut back on this expense, Coca-Cola launched New Coke as a diversion that would send consumers into a panic, spurring them to buy up all the remaining stock of the original formula. Then the company would "reconsider" its mistake, taking consumer discontent into serious consideration and relaunching what it could publicly state was the original formula—when it was really the newer, cheaper, corn syrup–laden recipe packed in the old can. And it gets more interesting: according to these conspiracy theorists, evidence that this was an inside job is that consumers can get the original formula, with sugar rather than corn syrup, at Passover each year, as corn is not kosher and so during that short period Coke reverts back to the sugary formula. How can one know this is the original formula? Conspiracy theorists argue that one can locate a "KP" or even Hebrew lettering somewhere on the can or bottle during Passover. The renewal of the brand's popularity comes by way of the publicity—however bad—of New Coke, and the subsequent relaunch, which stole the limelight from Pepsi during the seventy or so days New Coke was on the market.

Conspiracy theories aside, Coca-Cola's decision to change its formula was certainly grounded in a somewhat empirical popular experiment. Beginning in 1975, PepsiCo began a marketing campaign that featured a taste-test, offering consumers a single blind test in which they could deliberate upon which cola they found to be superior. Unsurprisingly—as PespiCo paid for and ran the commercials—Pepsi was showcased as the champion time and time again. Coca-Cola, for its part, had brand-name credibility, years of market share dominance, and a massive consumer following, but by the early 1980s Pepsi was right on its heels. According to an article in *Business Insider*, "Pepsi was enjoying popularity after successful marketing campaigns such as the 'taste test challenge' and 'Choice of a New Generation' featuring stars like singer Michael Jackson."[13]

It was becoming obvious that Pepsi had tapped into a young, vibrant, and much more participatory demographic, and Coca-Cola was scrambling to keep up. According to marketing expert Robert M. Schindler, it was the innovation of surveying public opinion that put the onus on Coca-Cola to respond:

> The campaign contributed to Coca-Cola's slow, but steady decline of market share in the soft-drink category. This erosion was most apparent

in food-store sales, which reflect consumer preferences more directly than do vending machine or fountain sales. By 1977, Pepsi had actually pulled ahead of Coke in food-store market share.[14]

The Coca-Cola Company was simply ill prepared to deal with the public campaign, and by 1985, the introduction of New Coke may have been the only card it had left to play.

Ultimately, bad publicity—brought about largely by Mullins—and public dissent forced the company to bring back its old formula. In a rather comical display of just how unpopular the popular American institution had become, ABC's Peter Jennings broke into a regularly scheduled television program to announce what Coca-Cola aficionados called the "second coming of Coke." As historian James Cobb recounts,

> Network executives had been understandably hesitant to interrupt the nation's most popular daytime soap opera. Yet viewers raised few complaints after ABC's Peter Jennings broke into *General Hospital*, on July 10, 1985, to tell them that, bowing to public outrage and stunned by the anemic sales figures of its replacement, Coca-Cola was moving to put its original soft-drink formula back on the market.[15]

If interrupting *General Hospital* were not enough, the company's president, Donald Keough, held a press conference the next day announcing the return of Coca-Cola's original formula. In what has been praised as a remarkable speech in its own right, Keough stated, "All of the time and money and skill that we poured into consumer research could not reveal the depth of feeling for the original taste of Coca-Cola," adding that "[s]ome cynics say we planned the whole thing. . . . The truth is we are not that dumb and we are not that smart."[16]

In the end, New Coke remained in niche markets in North America and US territories for nearly two more decades, even receiving a makeover and a new name—Coke II—in 1992. However, by July 2002, New Coke was discontinued altogether.

CHAPTER 9

Bud Dry

In April 1989, Anheuser-Busch introduced Bud Dry, a beer that offered one of the first popular compromises between traditional full-bodied brews and the increasingly trendy light brews. Bud Dry sprang on the drinking scene as an alternative's alternative—that is, the alternative to Anheuser-Busch's own Bud Light. It was positioned as another option for Anheuser-Busch loyalists, and it might have stood the test of time had it not mysteriously descended into the company of immemorable beverages. Was it an epic failure? Not at first, but the story of Bud Dry's gradual decline does provide something of a lesson in incremental downfalls.

As far as typical beers go, Bud Dry was actually quite a novelty. The caloric content was around 130 calories per eight-ounce bottle, just under the 145 calorie mark of a regular Budweiser and a bit heavier than the 110 calories of a Bud Light. The alcohol content was also relatively constant, at 5 percent, in contrast to anywhere between 4.5 and 5 percent in Bud Light. It seems that Bud Dry's brewmasters were able to pull off the same type of trick that makers of dry wine had done for centuries, allowing for less sugar and more alcohol per serving. *Diat Pils*, as dry beer is referred to in brewmaster parlance, is created by a process whereby brewers allow the yeast to consume virtually all the residual sugars and transform them into alcohol, resulting in a finish that doesn't cling to the palate like those that allow for such sugars to remain. Like the vast majority of Japanese beers, namely Asahi Dry, each drink is considered to be free of any real aftertaste.

Despite these innovations, Bud Dry essentially disappeared from the supermarket shelves and bar taps as early as 2006, and it was officially discontinued in 2010. Bearing the still somewhat coveted Anheuser-Busch logo and having fared rather well during its introduction, it seemed positioned to succeed, so what could have stopped Bud Dry in its tracks? Some theories point to marketing—especially the almost self-destructive, nonchalant catchphrase

Bud Dry's look and appeal had all the trappings of a great new addition to the Anheuser-Busch brand but virtually none of its success. ©*iStock/ monticelllo*

"Why ask why? Try Bud Dry"—which failed to ignite excitement among consumers. Other theories allude to an intrafamilial conflict between Bud Ice and Bud Dry, where the popularity of the former began to overshadow the latter to the point that consumers simply abandoned Bud Dry altogether. Still other theories suggest that the product itself may simply have been poorly conceived.

Exploring the first of these theories presents a mixed bag of hit-and-miss endeavors. Most of the content of the Bud Dry television commercials is in line with the times in which it was produced—the 1990s, when contrived irony, obnoxious slapstick, and hypermasculinity geared toward control, defamation, and sheer disrespect for females was in vogue in the world of marketing. For the latter reason in particular—and with all due respect to their producers—many of these advertisements are painful to watch on YouTube during the twenty-first century—something I endured for the research on this chapter. Nonetheless, these commercials are telling.

Each Bud Dry commercial generally includes three components: (1) the posing of grand, though not necessarily interesting questions; (2) some attempt at striking a comical chord with audiences by advocating indifference to such questions; and (3) a number of close-up, slow-motion images of an ice-cold (and often wet) Bud Dry bottle being popped open or draft being poured in a most melodramatic fashion. In combination, I suppose all three components melded together just fine, complementing one another in the thirty-second span of an advertisement. What more could one want in a beer commercial? After all, these commercials were intended to sell beer, not to become masterpieces of art, literature, or technology. Yet some critics directed their attention to the "Why ask why? Try Bud Dry" catchphrase that tied the components of the ads together.

So where did this problematic catchphrase originate? It was the brainchild of DDB Needham Worldwide—the same people who brought "Could've had a V8" and "Fahrvergnügen" into the public consciousness. There is no question that DDB Needham Worldwide had a great advertising pedigree, but perhaps that wasn't enough to launch a beer suffering from an identity crisis: launched after the popular images of Budweiser and Bud Light, yet in all respects characteristically *in between* the two. Perhaps what Bud Dry needed was a marketing campaign that was a bit more edgy and definitive, not a mediocre attempt at cleverness that ultimately suggested indecisiveness. In the end, isn't asking significant questions that won't be answered because they are almost immediately rendered insignificant kind of a lousy way to appease the curiosity of audiences? Bob Garfield, the celebrated columnist of *Advertising Age*, weighed in on this very question:

> What at first glance seems to be a celebration of critical thought—provocative questions about life's riddles, large and small—reveals itself to be Neanderthal in the extreme. The question in one spot may be posed as "Why do people hurt each other?" but ultimately, the question is "Why tax yourself dealing with troubling inquiry when you can be knocking back a cold one?"[1]

It seems that the whole idea of the advertisement centered more around the rhyme between asking why and trying Bud Dry,[2] as opposed to entertaining audiences with interesting ways to answer the questions initially posed. Quite frankly, the phrase suggests a rather aloof attitude in which the preference of beer need not matter, either.

To be fair, this was an experiment in cunning sales pitches, and going to these innovative lengths showed something akin to drive and ambition. Yet when one considers the audience—everyone from casual drinkers to bingers, or, really, anyone with access to a television—it isn't exactly a demographic that would be interested in big questions answered in thirty seconds, much less a group that needed to be reminded that it doesn't matter. As Garfield notes, "What better audience than the beer drinker to cultivate by ridiculing the idea of rigorous thought? What's ironic, though, is that the slogan's mnemonic and populist appeal are neutralized by the substance of the words themselves."[3]

What would have happened if these commercials had made an attempt at rigorous thought after all? Imagine a beer commercial in which the narrator realistically explores a question like: "How were the pyramids in Egypt constructed?" Perhaps there could be some short commentary, graphic animations, and concluding remarks about the falsifiabilty of the findings, to hold it to the fire of the scientific standards of inquiry. Oh—and of course the whole commercial could be sewn up with something like: "Aren't you glad we asked why? If so, try Bud Dry."

Of course, Anheuser-Busch is in the market of selling beer, not impressing upon audiences its ability to make great commercials. Yet by the summer of 1991, Anheuser-Busch reorganized some its marketing strategy by posing the "Why ask why?" question to women.[4] August Busch IV, then product manager of Bud Dry, stated that these commercials were prompted by letters from women who saw Bud Dry's previous advertising as chauvinistic. Garfield chimes in again on this point: "Clever advertising, price promotion, novelty and the sheer force of corporate will permit Bud Dry to flourish for a while, at the expense of other A-B brands. But then beer drinkers, nudged along by this advertising, will ask why, and the answer will be: No reason at all."[5]

To be certain, Bud Dry may have failed, but Anheuser-Busch did not. Roughly a decade after the introduction of Bud Dry, Anheuser-Busch and the two largest Brazilian brewing companies—Antarctica and Brahma—merged to form AmBev, establishing a footing that would lead an eventual run on the worldwide beer industry. Indeed, after a 2004 merger between AmBev and the Belgium-based Interbrew, the company became Anheuser-Busch InBev, which would go on to hold nearly a quarter of the entire market as of 2013—the largest share of the global beer market. So it is clear that the performance of one product does not necessarily define the potential of the company that produces it. Yet, why would company potential even be considered definable by merely one of the products it produces? Well, if one has learned anything from the attitude associated the marketing of Bud Dry, one simply needn't ask why.

CHAPTER 10

Crystal Pepsi

The year was 1992. The grunge look, casual chic, and styles running the gamut from denim shorts and fanny packs to baggy pants and sagging were in fashion. In music, it was basically Eric Clapton's year at the Grammy Awards—excluding, of course, Sir Mix-A-Lot's win for his absolutely genteel display of taste and charm in objectifying female derrieres in the song "Baby Got Back." In technology, the wide success of the compact disc hammered the last nail into the coffin of cassette tapes, and what we now refer to as the World Wide Web was introduced to the public, profoundly changing the face of information technology. In politics, President George H. W. Bush and Vice President Dan Quayle were scraping together the end of their first term in office, only a short time after we learned to "read lips" while watching taxes increase and were not-so-surprisingly reminded that there's no *e* in the word *potato*. The Cold War had come to an end, and for all intents and purposes, it was being gracefully swept under the rug of history—or, as Francis Fukuyama put it, "the end of history."

In addition to all this excitement, a well-publicized change took place in the soft-drink industry when PepsiCo decided to make transparency its top priority, losing the E150d caramel coloring and, on April 13, 1992, introducing Crystal Pepsi, marketed as a clear alternative to cola. The new drink was transparent and bubbly, appearing to be nothing short of refreshing. Pepsi's commercials featured impromptu scenes of consumers tasting Crystal Pepsi and commenting that it was "not as heavy," "not as syrupy," and—well, not the same as the traditional Pepsi they had come to know.

The new product was certainly not a remake of the old version, a scenario that would have been reminiscent of Coca-Cola's disastrous 1985 transformation to New Coke. Instead, Crystal Pepsi was not just a new look, it was actually a bit healthier, with no caffeine and 20 fewer calories per 12-ounce can than regular Pepsi.[1] All claims of novelty aside, however, colas had heretofore been

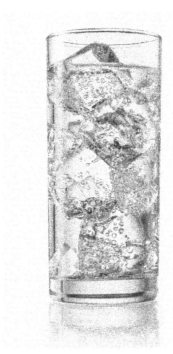

Crystal Pepsi on ice. ©*iStock/anna1311*

available only in various shades of brown, and changing that feature seemed to change the drink to something entirely different. It was almost as if association typologies began to emerge between colors and soft drinks: a green drink is Mountain Dew, an orange one is Crush or Cactus Cooler, a clear one has to be 7-Up or Sprite—and if it wasn't caramel brown, it wasn't a Pepsi. Yet PepsiCo ran with the idea and embarked upon a substantial marketing campaign, one that, above all other things, emphasized clarity.

With this, Pepsi was tapping into a pop cultural trend that included everything from detox and antioxidants to motivational seminars and health-kick fad diets. The evocative notion of transforming something that happened to be obscure into a something else that appeared to be some beacon of light was a rather crude way of fitting in with market trends—not to mention the political subtext that may have been stirring within the connotations surrounding dark versus light. But Pepsi was willing to take its chances, as marketing expert Matt Haig notes: "Both products [Crystal Pepsi and its diet version], Pepsi believed, answered the 'new consumer demand for purity.' After all this was a time when consumers were starting to opt for a bottle of Evian or Perrier just as often as they were picking up a bottle of Coke or Pepsi."[2]

Pepsi was riding the wave of a New Age health movement in which all things clear seemed to be equated with positive lifestyles, optimistic regard for adversity, and improving quality of life through a public display of transparent consumables. In many ways, one's commitment to all things clear suggested something about how *personally* clear one was. This didn't simply mean clearing up one's act with salads, plenty of rest, and exercise, but also utilizing products that were themselves clear. During this period, for example, Ivory Soap made the move from its classic milky-colored soap to a clear liquid[3] and the deodorant Mennen made a shift to Mennen Crystal Clean.[4] Indeed, even alcoholic beverages experimented clear products; as will be discussed in chapter 12, the American beer giant Coors set the bar for this trend when it introduced Zima, a clear alcoholic drink that dazzled drinkers with its bubbly look and just over 5 percent alcohol content. Coors also decided to take the ultimate step toward sobriety, edging in on the market for bottled water products by introducing Coors Rocky Mountain Sparkling Water.[5] After all, what could be clearer than water?

For the marketing of the Crystal Pepsi product, PepsiCo appeared to go a step beyond merely the fad of offering clear goods, developing the image of its new drink in such a way that seemed to cultivate a certain sense of social consciousness and responsibility. At no other time was this more apparent than when the company enlisted the popular band Van Halen, with its hit song "Right Now," for a Crystal Pepsi commercial that ran during a coveted Super Bowl halftime slot in 1993.

Similar to the official music video version, accompanied by singing from then–lead vocalist Sammy Hagar, the commercial featured a series of semi-thought-provoking phrases typed out across the screen, including, "Right now nature's inventing better stuff than science," "Right now only wildlife needs preservatives," and "Right now change is loose on the planet." Although the majority of these references complemented the social tenor of Van Halen's song, PepsiCo seized the moment by incorporating a few other references that conjured up a more explicit rendering of what Crystal Pepsi could offer: "Right now will do just fine without caffeine," "Right now we're all thirsty for something different," and "Right now is more refreshing than ever," aligning Crystal Pepsi with the newness and immediacy of the *now*. In a twist of irony, however, the *now* of the novel soft drink never really got off the ground and simply failed to generate a *later*. Despite a modicum of initial success, by late 1993 PepsiCo pulled the plug on the product and banished it—and all its clarity—into the depths with its other unsuccessful product lines.

With so much going for the new and innovative drink, it came as something of a surprise that Crystal Pepsi vanished. David Novak, chief operating officer of Pepsi-Cola North America and the real mastermind behind Crystal Pepsi, lamented the failure, but then chalked it up to a ride along the learning curve.

Just over a decade after PepsiCo closed down the operation, Novak reflected on his involvement:

> It was a tremendous learning experience. I still think it's the best idea I ever had, and the worst executed. A lot of times as a leader you think, "They don't get it; they don't see my vision." People were saying we should stop and address some issues along the way, and they were right. It would have been nice if I'd made sure the product tasted good. Once you have a great idea and you blow it, you don't get a chance to resurrect it.[6]

Not withstanding Novak's candid hindsight, perhaps he may have taken too much of the fall for a product that simply didn't survive in the industry.

To be clear, the entire soft-drink industry is full of missteps and false starts—Crystal Pepsi is only one of them. Market-share king Coca-Cola, for example, made a similar, though much more measured move by responding to Pepsi with the introduction of Tab Clear.[7] Indeed, within only a couple years of its introduction, Tab Clear joined Crystal Pepsi and fell by the cola industry wayside.

So what actually happened to Crystal Pepsi? Some experts blamed consumers' confusion and their inability to make the connection between a taste and a color didn't seem to go together: "The colorless, caffeine-free cola failed to become popular because many people could not make the connection between the cola's colorlessness and its taste. It was difficult for consumers to imagine a cola being clear, and some even claimed it tasted like lemon-lime soda."[8]

There's certainly some substance to this claim; after all, we as consumers often come to establish our loyalty to certain items based upon the images they create for us through a host of referents, not the least of which is appearance. Often when a product rises to even modest levels of success, its appearance becomes a reference enmeshed within an economy of other product references—held to the standards of successes associated with other successful products marketed by the same company. The referents that contribute to a product's popular identification are not confined to a one-time encounter with it, but instead the product's reputation is built upon a whole series of sensual experiences that establish recognition. Take, for example, popular automobile brands. The visual emblems of Mercedes-Benz, BMW, and Volkswagen that adorn the hoods of these automobiles are symbols that distinguish their brand names from others as well as referents that grow to become signifiers associated with the experience of driving quality cars. This experience is not a drive down the road, but is related to the way the car handles, smells, feels, and so on. Over time, the combination of these experiences conjures up certain perceptions about what this product offers to its consumers. With the formation of these commodity typecasts, the effect of changing any part of the product—especially its appearance—can be devastating.

In a similar, slightly nuanced version of this, others have attributed the failure of Crystal Pepsi not to a state of confusion about the product and its image, but instead to unfulfilled expectations informed by connotative meanings. Lawrence L. Garber Jr., Eva M. Hyatt, and Richard G. Starr Jr. explain:

> Apart from its clear color, Crystal Pepsi was identical to regular Pepsi in all other respects, including flavor. However, Pepsico failed to consider the possibility of a food color/flavor interaction with dire consequences. To cola drinkers, clearness connoted certain "non-cola" flavor expectations. Consequently, cola drinkers trying Crystal Pepsi for the first time were bowled over by its full flavor. Even most regular Pepsi Cola drinkers didn't like it.[9]

According to this line of thinking, the taste experience of Crystal Pepsi may have been confounded by a disjunction between preconceived expectations and the actual experience. Although the look was different, the taste was not, leaving expectations unfulfilled.

In another example, when 7-Up was introduced during the first quarter of the twentieth century, its originators also had to grapple with consumer expectations. In fact, the original 7-Up had caramel coloring, and the "brown lemon-lime drink" wasn't received very well.[10] In this instance, it seems that consumers were more interested in the continuity between the look of the citrus juice ingredient and the look of the output they would drink.

The relationship between color and flavor is a peculiar one. A whole body of literature dating back to the early days of modern marketing has repeatedly emphasized this point. Indeed, it appears that the way in which individuals process flavors and recognize various tastes can actually be dependent upon color—something that has no flavor at all. Celebrated food market researcher Howard R. Moskowitz has elaborated on this point several times. As he notes, "[C]olors influence the initial visual judgments of foods, and provide sensory information that either reinforces or conflicts with taste and smell inputs."[11] Moskowitz goes on to discuss a telling experiment that illustrates this point:

> Moir prepared a buffet of foods for a dinner with scientific colleagues of the Flavor Group of the Society of Chemistry and Industry in London. Many of the foods were inappropriately colored, and during the dinner several individuals complained about the off-flavor of many of the foods served. Several of the individuals reported feeling ill after eating some of the foods, despite the fact that only the color was varied. The rest of the food was perfectly wholesome, with the requisite taste, smell and texture.[12]

It would thus seem that the representation of color in tandem with flavor may engender something of a psychosomatic condition. Yet notwithstanding these interesting notions of what we might call a psychology of taste, I believe there may be something far more critical missing among these explanations: the general ebb and flow of a product's popularity.

Given that Crystal Pepsi was introduced at a time when the popularity of all things clear—both material and nonmaterial—was so high, why didn't the timing propel it into the world of everyday consumable products for years to come? Why didn't it evolve to meet consumer demands? Perhaps a failure of this sort could be better attributed to something a bit more abstract—like, say, cultural evolution. In other words, as incredible as the potential was for Crystal Pepsi to make it big, it simply did not survive, and this may be due to the fact that it lacked enough willing catalysts—that is, consumers—to maintain its life. At the risk of being misunderstood and accused of venturing into the world of science fiction, I should add that the success or failure of a product may be connected to how well it implants itself in our minds.

In 1976 Richard Dawkins published *The Selfish Gene*, a treatise on a theory of gene-centered evolution. Unlike Charles Darwin's work, which focused on the individual as the unit of analysis for evolution through natural selection, Dawkins substitutes this focus with the gene as the central evolutionary unit. For Dawkins, genes and their successful proliferation, and thus their prosperity, are key to their survival.

To explain, think of genes as parts of an instruction manual—like, for instance, the recipe for baking a pastry—torn into small bits and pieces of paper. Each of these bits and pieces contains part of the necessary information that explains how the different ingredients must be handled and mixed, and when these bits and pieces are correctly reassembled, successfully brought to the fore, and replicated over time, the pastries they produce, like individuals, survive. We, however, are merely vessels for our genes, and when we die the vessel that carries these genes is disposed of; if we somehow reproduce, however, we then pass on our genes to another generation. So, in this scenario, it is not *we* that survive, but the *genes* we carry. In this way, the phrase *selfish gene* does not suggest that genes, or even the individuals that carry them, are somehow selfish (though they may very well be in some fantastic kind of way); instead, it means that genes that survive and thrive through a new generation are those that have looked after themselves and their own self-interests.

Dawkins, however, steps beyond the biological concepts of gene and applies this evolutionary model to cultural contexts. Arguing that genes are the dominant replicating entities of our planet, Dawkins intimates that, like the inception of life within a primordial soup, we are also constantly immersed within another life-generating soup composed of culture rather than chemical compounds. It is in this soup—best thought of as interaction, whether face-to-face or via other technological mediums—that ideas are copied and reproduced in light of their cultural functions. Slightly corrupting the Greek term for imitation, *mīmēmia*, Dawkins introduces the cultural version of a gene which he calls a *meme*—those items of cultural transmission that allow for others to imitate. As Dawkins notes,

> Examples of memes are tunes, ideas, catch-phrases, clothes fashions, ways of making pots or of building arches. Just as genes propagate themselves in the gene pool by leaping from body to body via sperms or eggs, so memes propagate themselves in the meme pool by leap-ing from brain to brain via a process which, in the broad sense, can be called imitation. If a scientist hears, or reads about, a good idea, he passes it on to his colleagues and students. He mentions it in his articles and his lectures. If the idea catches on, it can be said to propa-gate itself, spreading from brain to brain.[13]

Thus memes take hold of our sense of what merits replication. Memes do not do so by taking us hostage (at least not in a violent way), but instead by occupy-ing our minds in such a way that they convince us of the necessity to reproduce them. So, in many ways, we become hosts for memes, assisting them in their survival insofar as other individuals begin to view their merits in the same light and imitate them.

Take language, for example: the success of living languages versus the failure of those languages that have died off. There are multiple variations in languages, all struggling for survival in a volatile world of competition, and those that have adapted to other evolving social conditions have successfully sustained themselves over time—although languages themselves did nothing by themselves! In other words, living languages have propagated themselves through the minds of individuals, as they have been present among humans who carried them all over the world, resulting in a subtle and perhaps taken-for-granted adaptation.

Ideas and their potential to become popular may be viewed through this type of replicating schema. As explained in a 2002 TED Talk by the American philosopher Daniel Dennett, the notion that ideas can also hijack the mind is a rather interesting argument. As Dennett notes: "A virus is a string of nucleic acid with attitude. That is that something about it that tends to make it repli-cate better than the competition does; and that's what a meme is, a meme is an information packet with attitude."[14] Dennett's use of the term *attitude* here is not merely a strategy to draw attention to the fact that memes, like viruses, are not simply inconsequential, but instead it appears that he does so to highlight that they are animated entities that inculcate the minds of humans in spite of humans themselves.

In a telling example of how memes may be thought of as even more con-sequential than biological viruses, Dennett highlights a case where a faith-based movement failed to survive due not to some plague, but rather to a cultural deficiency where a meme died out. Dennett explains this point through the example of the the Shakers—the late eighteenth-century religious movement known for dynamic devotional rituals, furniture craft, and, above all, a strict tenet of celibacy. Dennett emphasizes that with this celibacy, it might follow that the Shakers' demise could be chalked up to an impossibility of evolution due to the proscription of sex, yet the Shakers were unique in this regard, as they had plenty of potential converts: the lack of social welfare programs at the time generated an abundance of orphans, to whom the Shakers proselytized. In this way, the downfall of the first wave of Shakers was not a necessarily attributable to the absence of the procreation so vital to the evolution of humans, but instead to a meme-like concept of religious faith that failed to replicate.

Crystal Pepsi can also be thought of as a meme: a concept that possessed a great deal of potential during a time when the notion of clarity was seemingly ev-erywhere. Yet the flood of other soft drinks, including Coca-Cola, Pepsi, 7-Up, and the like, were already meeting the demand, and introducing a new concept that had to compete in this market really amounted to a sink-or-swim scenario. Along this line of reasoning, the failure of the Crystal Pepsi meme was that it simply didn't latch on and replicate itself in the same fashion that the standard darker colas and the already established clear drinks had. Ultimately, Crystal Pepsi's playful marketing tagline—"You've never seen a taste like this"—spoke volumes about how the clarity of the soft drink may have actually rendered it, and its taste, invisible!

CHAPTER 11

Burger King's Table Service

Fast food, as its name suggests, is food that can be prepared, consumed, and even discarded at an accelerated pace. For many Americans, the combination of hamburgers, French fries, and soft drinks has come to embody the standard fast-food meal accompanied by such social amenities as practicality, convenience, inexpensiveness, and, in general, the satisfactory experience of moving from being hungry to being full. Unlike more traditional restaurants in which dining entails being seated by a host and waited on by servers—and often spending a reasonable amount of time and money—the fast-food model operates in a much more streamlined fashion.

In the United States there is certainly no shortage of fast-food establishments, and the formula for accommodating the dietary needs of individuals on the go has been a rather successful one. But when fast-food establishments move beyond the model of providing customers food without the frills of traditional restaurants, they risk compromising that success and reaping the consequences of failure.

In 1991 the fast-food giant Burger King introduced table service, a rare innovation designed to give the customer a warm welcome and perhaps evoke the feelings of comfort associated with restaurant dinning. Offered between the hours of 4:00 and 8:00 pm, table service included the delivery of customers' orders, free popcorn, crayons, coloring page tray liners, and the addition of a few more upscale menu items, including fried shrimp, chicken fillet, and even a steak sandwich—albeit with a ground-beef patty in place of actual steak. While these meals were also served with condiments, flatware, and napkins, some franchises went even further to enrich the setting; one spokesman commented that some restaurants would "change the ambiance at dinner by using tablecloths, playing music and dimming the lights."[1] Additionally, in an effort to demonstrate the attention Burger King paid to its clientele, servers made visits to the tables, checking on customers' satisfaction and, in many cases, bussing tables at the end of meals. Finally, despite the custom of showing gratitude for such service, it was Burger King's policy to forbid tips.

Not surprisingly, Burger King's table service was initially well received, especially in pilot runs prior to the official launch.[2] Why *wouldn't* one want to be waited on, as opposed to having to go the extra mile to do it for oneself? Moreover, the free popcorn alone—as a subsidy to an already cheap dining experience—must have appealed to the majority of customers. Yet within no time at all, Burger King terminated the service and went back to the do-it-yourself model.

So why did table service fail to launch? Did Burger King workers complain about extra responsibilities without tips? Were the customers somehow confused about table service at a fast-food restaurant? Perhaps they viewed Burger King employees approaching the dining table as too intrusive—or, conversely, maybe the service was fine, but the four-hour window was far too limited. Undoubtedly the problem couldn't have been the free popcorn!

Table service took the efficiency out of fast-food dining, slowing down the whole objective of an expedient means-to-ends process. ©iStock/Zurijeta

Notwithstanding these and other more pragmatic factors—not the least of which was the bottom line—the failure of table service may have been linked to something more discreet, like irrationality. In many ways, the implementation of table service was an attempt to bring the irrationally slow pace of dining in the convenience of one's home into the rationalized world of the fast-food dining experience. Yet in doing so, Burger King may have broken one of the fundamental, though unspoken, rules of the rationality model: making things run more efficiently by making them run faster. Indeed, as I demonstrate in this chapter, Burger King's table service failure had less to do with the reception of its innovative move toward setting and serving the table and more to do with the fact that its service interfered with getting customers in and out of the restaurant rationally.

The late nineteenth- and early twentieth-century social theorist Max Weber was quite familiar with models of rationality. In an extensive critique of bureaucratic systems that runs throughout much of his work, Weber argues that the formal rationalization that is sought after and exercised in an attempt to achieve an optimal means-to-ends enterprise may not necessarily produce positive outcomes. Although Weber acknowledges the benefits of formal rationalization, he is leery of how such a process may dehumanize the individuals who operate within its strictures. In other words, emphasizing sets of ideal standards and procedures to meet a given goal can have the latent effect of removing the creative qualities of individuals and even locking them into a world of rather dull and generally foreseeable lives—or, as Weber argues, a state of social disenchantment.

In one of the most creative and innovative applications of social theory to modernity, sociologist George Ritzer has reintroduced Weber's ideas through the fast-food industry phenomenon. For Ritzer, the model through which fast-food establishments operate serves as a rather profound example of formal rationalization in the twentieth and twenty-first centuries. Referring to his theoretical concept as the "McDonaldization of Society," Ritzer argues that the type of rationalization that Weber so unnervingly observed has emerged as the dominant form of social organization. As Ritzer explains, McDonaldization is "the process by which the principles of the fast-food restaurant are coming to dominate more and more sectors of American society as well as the rest of the world."[3]

Taking cues from Weber's work, Ritzer outlines the four dimensions of rationalization as they apply to the fast-food industry. These dimensions include efficiency (the streamlining of a process), calculability (the quantification of products and productions), predictability (the recognized standardization of products and productions), and control through nonhuman technology (the substitution of human activity with nonhuman innovation). In combination, these features engender rationality; yet, as Ritzer argues, this rigid form of rationalization emerges at the expense of human creativity and may ultimately produce irrational outcomes.

So what does all this talk of rationality, irrationality, and the like have to do with the introduction and subsequent failure of Burger King's table service? Well, to be frank, just about everything, as it would appear that Burger King made too many irrational moves too quickly. For Weber—and, by extension, for Ritzer—rational projects inevitably generate irrational ends; one need not help this process along. In other words, prematurely introducing an irrational segment of a rational project before the whole enterprise becomes irrational is kind of like doubling the odds of failure against itself.

Although this may sound confusing, a little explanation of how rational processes give way to irrational processes may be helpful. To begin, let's consider efficiency and its ubiquity throughout the fast-food restaurant industry. From the assembly-line method of piecing together hamburgers to the introduction (and success) of the drive-through, the experience of dining at a fast-food restaurant is anything but inefficient. According to Ritzer, one example of Burger King's operation actually defines this well: "The ultimate application of the assembly line to the fast-food process is Burger King's conveyor belt: A raw, frozen hamburger placed on one end moves slowly via the conveyor under a flame and emerges in ninety-four seconds on the other end fully cooked."[4]

But despite making Ritzer's list of rational examples used to introduce the feature of efficiency, the Burger King conveyor belt is also an object of irrationality. Although efficient, the assembly-line method runs in stark contrast to the "Your Way, Right Away" motto; in actuality, you can only have it the way the conveyor belt cooks it. All the imagined burger autonomy in the world won't stop the conveyor belt for any one customer's input; instead, the efficiency of assembly lines literally reduces creative options to a minimum—if not erasing options all together. Similar to Henry Ford's comment that customers could have the Model T in "any color . . . so long as it's black," Burger King's efficiency serves to streamline enough items that variation—even at the request of the customer—is difficult to come by.

The second feature of McDonaldization—calculability—is equally ubiquitous among fast-food establishments. As Ritzer explains,

> Quantity tends to become a surrogate for quality. Numerical standards are set for both processes (production, for example) and end results (goods, for example). In terms of processes, the emphasis is on speed (usually high), whereas for end results, the focus is on the number of products produced and served or on their size (usually large).[5]

Quantifying everything from timing and temperature to the number of burgers sold and measurable amounts of condiments makes the world of fast-food restaurants a real balance-sheet-like operation. Emphasizing this quantification certainly paints a clear picture of the comings and goings of inventory drawn from calculated expenses and revenue, yet what does this feature of rationality do for customers? Despite the solid numerical expressions through which bookkeeping can be handled, this kind of extensive quantification serves to reduce the human qualities transferred into the product to the extent that only numbers count. According to Ritzer,

> The emphasis on quantity tends to affect adversely the quality of both the process and the result. For customers, calculability often means eating on the run (hardly a "quality" dining experiences) and consuming food that is almost always mediocre. For employees, calculability often means obtaining little or no personal meaning from their work; therefore, the work products, and service suffer.[6]

In this way, quality is constantly being sacrificed for quantity, making for a rather average dining experience.

Predictability, the third feature of McDonaldization refers to the fulfillment of expectations in a seemingly natural fashion. In other words, products are always made in such a way that they appear the same everywhere: a McDonald's cheeseburger in Tokyo looks just like a McDonald's cheeseburger in Brussels, French fries in Paris are the same as French fries in New York, and so on. Predictability, however, serves several functions, not the least of which is reducing the effort put forth to create, experience, and even identify that which we encounter. As Ritzer notes,

> From the consumer's point of view, predictability makes for much peace of mind in day-to-day dealings. For workers, predictability makes tasks easier. In fact, some workers prefer effortless, mindless, repetitive work because, if nothing else, it allows them to think of other things, even daydream, while they are doing their tasks.[7]

As predictability increases, the dining experience and all the products one consumes or interacts with while dining become standardized and uniform. In an enterprise oriented toward serving the wishes of large numbers of people, the only thing that can really accommodate as many customers as possible is compromise through variation. Yet the feature of predictability, so vital to the rational process, cannot allow for variation, much less surprises that deviate from this model, making for a pretty commonplace experience.

Finally, the fourth feature of McDonalidization—control through nonhuman technology—refers to the substitution or replacement of human capacities with nonhuman technologies. In this definition technology includes "not only machines and tools but also materials, skills, knowledge, rules, regulations, procedures, and techniques."[8] In this way, everything—from the operations manual of a bureaucratic corporation that lays down the law and the colorful pictographic guidelines for assembling a hamburger, to corralling and ushering automobiles past the drive-through window and the visibility of the trash receptacles that subtly admonish costumers to bus their own tables—is considered a mechanism of control. As Ritzer explains, humans make up the vast majority of unpredictable outcomes, erring along the learning curve; thus the incorporation of control through nonhuman technology is thought to minimize mistakes and generate a more smooth-running operation. It almost goes without saying, however, that replacing people, formal rules, regulations, and automated machinery undermine human potential.

On the surface, each of these features appears to make fast-food restaurants operate in a much more streamlined fashion that not only saves money and time, but also prevent against unanticipated consequences. Yet, in accordance with Weber's reservations, these features of rationality often generate irrational outcomes.[9]

For Ritzer, irrationalization of rational processes connotes the negative aspects of McDonaldization, or that which contradicts the intended purposes of a given rational enterprise. As he notes, "[R]ational systems are unreasonable systems that deny humanity, the human reason, of the people who work within them or are served by them."[10] These irrationalities are, in a word, dehumanizing. In this way, the rigid control of the entire fast-food enterprise suggests a subtle suppression of individuals' capacities to be creative. To be fair, fast-food restaurants need not incorporate extensive creativity in order to be successful. Yet if the success stories of the fast-food industry tell us anything about the necessary formula for accomplishments, fostering the four features of rationality is a must.

As we've seen above, rationality inevitably gives way to irrationality, but that doesn't necessarily suggest failure—quite the contrary, in fact, as small amounts of irrationality at the end of a profitable day may bode well for a restaurant, especially when business owners can capitalize on these shortcomings in terms of cutting costs and when customers are willing to get what they perceive they've paid for. However, being too risky or too innovative, too fast, can contribute to the demise of such an enterprise.

If this is so, how then did Burger King's table service induce premature irrationality? To begin, table service was highly inefficient. As the primary goal of efficiency is to increase the pace at which solutions are arrived at—in this case, feeding customers and sending them on their way—table service did the opposite by slowing down the whole process. Whereas in the counter-service model, the employee's duties end after handing the meal off to the customers, the table-service model extends this period of duty and even adds the additional steps of checking on customer satisfaction and then bussing and cleaning the dirty tables.

Table service also ran counter to efficiency in another way: through disrupting the otherwise brief commitment to the deliverable. This model draws employees out from behind the counter in the service of the customers, and depending on the volume of orders, delivering the meals on trays puts the employees at risk of physical encounters while crisscrossing the obstacle course of other employees, customers, and stable fixtures in search of the guest.

Burger King's table service was also a true contradiction of calculability. At the turn of the twentieth century, the American engineer Frederick Winslow Taylor set out to establish the "one best way"—the most efficient method of executing a particular venture. In arriving at this method, Taylor initiated his "time and motion studies," wherein he literally timed the movements of industrial coal and steel workers, assessing the necessity of their actions, and ultimately eliminating steps that were determined to be unnecessary. Known today as Taylorism, this systematic method has had a profound impact on everything from telephone switchboard operations and automobile assembly to the organization of the modern household kitchen—and the inner workings of the fast-food industry. Despite the complexities of the research Taylor used to arrive at his ideal methods, his one weapon safeguarding necessary movements was a simple stopwatch—a pillar of calculability.

Though it's just a hunch, I would venture to guess that Taylor would have seen Burger King's table service as a disaster in terms of time and motion. Not only was the service a needless waste of time that might have been better spent on other restaurant tasks, it also created a series of unnecessary steps. Above all, it would have been difficult for Taylor to thoroughly measure the calculable loss of both time and motion that table service generated for a number of reasons—not the least of which being that it undoubtedly would have been eliminated in the planning stages.

Burger King's table service also ran contrary to the rational feature of predictability. While on the surface, between the hours of 4:00 and 8:00 pm, customers could expect to be welcomed by the free popcorn and an enhanced menu, could the same be said for the actual service itself? Even within restaurants where waitresses and waiters undergo training, the service often becomes the object of a complaint. For Burger King servers, left to their own devices and well aware that they'll receive no tips for their extra efforts, it's anyone's guess how consistently they conformed to the predictable hospitality of table service.

Finally, table service at Burger King threatened no other feature of rationality more than control through nonhuman technology. As one of the justifications for implementing mechanisms of nonhuman technology is to minimize the unpredictability of human error, table service plainly renders this reasoning null. Allowing customers to handle their own items from order to consumption, then subtly directing the discarding of rubbish, removes accountability for error from

Burger King employees; table service works in the reverse, placing that account-ability back on the employees.

Burger King's table service, however, was an instance where a restaurant fought *against* this irrationality by manufacturing it before it played its course. In other words, by disregarding how the model for fast-food establishments functions, then incorporating a more personalized feature for its customers, Burger King created a form of irrationality that didn't quite conform to the ir-rationalities that such systems are so often inclined to accept—those being the minimal irrationalities generated by the four features of rationalization. It seems that going out of the way to make customers feel more welcome challenges the notion of assisting them in quickly moving from a state of hunger to a state of satisfaction. As ironic as it may seem, inefficiency, unpredictability, incalculabil-ity, and uncontrollability may compromise quality dining, yet such compromise may be the very thing that both owners and customers of fast-food establish-ments anticipate and are willing to experience in such settings.

Ultimately, Burger King should be noted for its innovation, as its table service was perhaps less of a failure than one may presume, and it may be more insightful to see this venture as an amenity whose time had not yet come. In fact, as the model for fast-food operations adapts to new technologies—in particular, offering such communication technology as free Wi-Fi[11]—it seems apparent that a variety of features bound to the rational model will have to give up some ground. For example, in 2011 some French McDonald's franchises found suc-cess in testing table service, including "card remote tactile screens" for making purchases from the convenience of the dining table.[12]

Ritzer himself recognizes that some deviations from the rational model have been quite successful.[13] Starbucks, for instance, has successfully deviated from the fast-food (or fast-coffee) model by cleverly offering a place for customers to relax and enjoy their surroundings—although unbeknownst to them, or perhaps at their indifference, the customers themselves then become informal props that onlookers associate with the Starbucks experience.

In addition to the changes these other service industry businesses are mak-ing, Burger King appears to be falling in line with important adaptations. In 2012 Burger King announced that it would provide a delivery service to custom-ers in select areas for a nominal fee.[14] According to the company's website, by the end of 2012 Burger King delivery service was available at dozens of restaurants in Florida, Maryland, Virginia, New York, and Texas.[15] Although only time will tell whether this new innovation will succeed or fail, if the success of the pizza delivery model is any indication of things to come, Burger King may be on to something. With the failure of table service behind it, perhaps new innovation along these lines is just what Burger King needs.

CHAPTER 12

Zima

In 1993 the Coors Brewing Company introduced Zima, a charcoal-filtered low-grade lager that looked and tasted nothing like beer. The product's name was the brainchild of a rather successful outfit that would later give birth to some notable branding in the world of computer technology: "According to its coiners at Lexicon Branding, Inc. (also the creators of such high-profile brands as Intel's Pentium Chip and the Apple PowerBook notebook computer), zima is the Russian word for 'winter,' a good match for a cold, clear beverage that resembled vodka."[1]

In addition to the clever name, Zima's distinction as a non-beer beer was a somewhat exciting novelty. Much of Zima's dissimilarity to traditional beer was due to its unique filtering process, which literally rendered it colorless and tasteless—except, of course, for the added artificial citrus flavor. Additionally, when poured, Zima was headless, which removed one of the very visible characteristics that makes a beer—well, a *beer*. Presumably this was fine, as Coors marketed the beverage as an alternative to beer: as several of its commercials in the 1990s claimed, Zima was "Zomething Different."

Consumers, however, weren't quite sure what to make of Zima. Although it was certainly different, was it still a beer, or even beer-like? If not, was it a wine? If so, could it be considered a wine cooler or more similar to other popular fizzy "alcopop" drinks? Consumer response on the matter was pretty clear, claiming that Zima tasted like a citrusy wine spritzer, and with its 5.4 percent alcohol content at the time of its commercial release, the debate was pretty much settled: Zima was a beer that looked like seltzer water and tasted like a bubbly citrus drink. In a peculiar fashion, this deviation from the traditional look and taste of beer made Zima unfitting of the criteria for a "man's beer," which at the time ran the gamut from light yellow lagers to heavy amber-colored ales and full-bodied black porters and stouts. It followed that Zima failed to entice males, the main beer-drinking demographic that drives the industry.

Despite its eventual failure, however Zima made an excellent run, especially because it was able to ride the wave of the clarity movement that was in vogue at the time. That is, during the early 1990s, a real emphasis on all things "clear" swept through the marketing industry. For example, Ivory Soap transformed from its milky-white look to a clear liquid soap[2] and Mennen deodorant went transparent as well with its Mennen Crystal Clean deodorant.

In addition to soaps and deodorants, major soft-drink companies fell in line with this novel concept of clear. In fact, PepsiCo made two attempts in the 1990s with its Crystal Pepsi and Crystal from Pepsi products, and Coca-Cola took a shot at it as well with its Tab Clear drink. Needless to say, both companies discontinued these products shortly after their respective introductions.

Other beer companies also experimented with clear product creations. Pabst briefly marketed Izen Klar[3] and Strohs went a similar route with Strohs Clash[4]—both short-lived drinks that were proved to be similar failed-beer innovations. Even Miller, the former rival turned partner of Coors, marketed a clear beer known as Miller Clear, which was abandoned in 1993 after initial test trials indicated that projections for a future market looked grim.[5]

Zima on ice may have been a clear alternative to colorful, rich, frothy beers, yet its transparency seemed to confuse consumers and failed to draw a faithful following of alcohol drinkers. ©*iStock/bhofack2*

But Zima seemed to have it made, as it really *was* something different. Zima's marketing team made every effort to give it an edge on the competition, and to this end it was initially rather well received. To illustrate, many beer advertisements at the time were centered on the image of hardworking men winding down with their pals over cold beers and playfully scheming ways to attract women. Many Zima commercials, however, featured a young, mellow-mannered Roger Kabler in a loose-fitting suit and his signature fedora. Unlike the brutish males of traditional beer commercials, Kabler had a relaxed appeal, charming his company and conveying a certain degree of sophistication by encouraging consumers to take a chance on the new beverage, which might change the way they viewed their drinking environment—and themselves.

Kabler's performance wasn't entirely without the quirky marketing gimmicks of the 1990s. Zima capitalized on the infrequent appearance of the letter *Z*, using it as a substitute for every *S* that left Kabler's mouth: "*Zo*, you're all *zet* for a barbecue," "*It'z* not like beer, you *zee*, no *zuds*," and "Not *zo zweet*, try a *zip.*" These advertisements were eventually phased out and replaced with ones that resembled other popular beer commercials of the time.

As the popularity of Zima dwindled, and still trying to draw in male consumers, marketers reverted to the advertising model of "drink this and you'll get that"—*that*, of course, being a female. In one Zima commercial set in a bowling alley, the protagonist is faced with three beverage options: a beer, a Smirnoff Ice knockoff, and a Zima. Grabbing hold of each one separately, the actor experiences a vision of what each drink will bring him. His first choice, a beer, conjures up a scene of an elderly man bowling with the aid of his walker; his second choice, the Smirnoff Ice knockoff, brings to mind the company of swanky and indifferent-mannered males, preoccupied with their cell phones rather than their company. Touching the Zima, however, evokes the image of several women dressed in pink nighties and slippers, bowling under the falling feathers from a pillow fight. The upshot is that Zima—or, as it is called in the commercial, "Plan Z"—is the exciting alternative, suggesting that the drink moved the young bowler one step closer to jumping into bed with playful and energetic women. But the apparent shift in advertising strategy did not make much difference; consumers still weren't purchasing Zima at a rate that yielded a profitable return.

If the ineffectiveness of Zima's commercials wasn't bad enough, the unanticipated result of an odd sociocultural phenomenon known as *rumor* contributed to Zima's downfall. As a mix of urban legends and flat-out criticism began to circulate, Zima became the focus of several rumors, including that it had been specially formulated to aid weight loss and, to the legal detriment of some believers, that it contained a rare chemical formula that was undetectable by a Breathalyzer. Neither of these rumors helped Zima's image when frequent drinkers began to gain weight and drunk-on-Zima drivers racked up DUI charges. Coming of age during Zima's marketing blitz, I remember a number of these rumors. My favorite, in contrast to the one about weight loss, was that Zima's contents—mostly some unpronounceable chemical that roughly rhymed with Zima—would, over time, solidify as an amorphous rubbery mass in one's stomach, leading to rapid weight gain. For young people new to drinking, this may have been a rather convenient explanation for packing on the pounds.

Notwithstanding the circulation of rumors, Zima was destined for doom for yet another reason. As if Strother Martin himself emerged from the grave to reenact his famous line from *Cool Hand Luke*—holding a Zima in hand and proclaiming, "What we've got here is failure to communicate"—Zima had sent the wrong message. Indeed, a beer intended for men had defied expectations and crossed over as a preferred drink among women.

Critics of Zima weighed in early on this point, finding themselves just as confused about its identity as consumers were. Some tortured the beverage through explicit emasculation, depicting it as a lesser choice for the "manly" activity of drinking. As Brendan Koerner comments in *Slate*,

> There are a million ways to slight a rival's manhood, but to suggest that he enjoys Zima is one of the worst. Zima was the original "malternative"—a family of alcoholic beverages that eventually came to include such abominations as Smirnoff Ice and Bacardi Silver— and it has long been considered the very opposite of macho: a drink that fragile coeds swill while giving each other pedicures.[6]

It seems that the flashy look of Zima's transparency, bubbles, and stylized label broke too far from conventional norms associated with male-oriented drinks. Yet this failure was not due to lack of effort, as Koerner parenthetically noted: "(Coors pointedly instructed stores to never place Zima alongside wine coolers, which male drinkers regard as effete)."[7]

With well-intentioned commercials failing to reach audiences and rumors abounding about how beneficial (or even detrimental) the drink actually was, the straw that broke the camel's back came down to the public perception of Zima as defying gender roles. But how can a product be considered to be gendered, much less accommodating such vague notions of gender roles? One might be surprised.

Although most consumable products appear to be inanimate without the assistance of human interaction, this does not necessarily suggest that consumer perception of their positions and places in society are beyond the forces of the social process known as *labeling*. Beer can assume a variety of labels, some of which are entwined with gender: Take, for instance, Stone Brewing's Arrogant Bastard Ale, which smacks of a hypermasculinity, or the voyeuristic marketing gimmick from Golden Beverages' Nude Beer, featuring labels with women in bikinis—which, of course, could be scratched off, revealing something rather telling about both the taste of the beer and the beer drinker who consumes it.

Beers like these have certain gender associations that may be used first and foremost for marketing, but which also convey something about the significance of beer in modern society. As one critic notes, "Between 1969 and 1971, several breweries produced 'alcoholic soda pops' that were the beer equivalent of the successful wine coolers. There was Hamm's Right Time Red, with a sweet, cherry flavor for females who wanted to get fruit looped, and Right Time Gold, with a tart grapefruit taste for the guys."[8] Indeed, beer, like a lot of products, is anything but asexual, and the innovation and failure of Zima was no exception.

The world of gender construction is a complex one. Unlike biological sex, which has rather strict parameters designating what constitutes a male or a female through anatomical constructs and chromosomal makeup, gender categories have never been definitive. Although not conducive to fair and just gender relations in the development of life cycles, male children are often socialized to be aggressive, adventurous, and forthcoming, while female children are socialized to be passive, cautious, and nurturing—running parallel to the old nursery rhyme that says boys are made of "slugs and snails and puppy dogs' tails," while girls are made of "sugar and spice and everything nice." The profit motive bound to capitalism has exploited these gendered assumptions and forcefully established market segmentation, making different products for males and females while appending gender stereotypes to each in an attempt to tap into psychology of consumers.

Nevertheless, the arbitrariness of gender does not belie the fact that individuals have gone to great lengths to make certain associations, expressions, practices, and even objects strictly male or female. When these categorical perceptions run wild in the world of consumption, some products run the risk of falling susceptible to market expectations that fail to justify their survival; although it may seem promising to target one gender for the sale of a given product, doing so can make any deviation from this intended target audience a real kiss of death.

One product that has an exclusive association with a particular gender is the urinal. It's practical, convenient, and appears to be aligned with all notions of a happy marriage between form and function. Yet women have also sought to make this amenity a part of their lifestyle. In fact, during the early 1990s, a Florida-based company introduced the She-inal, a female urinal designed to provide women with the convenience of standing while urinating. It even had some takers: at one point the management of Baltimore's Oriole Park at Camden Yards contemplated making the She-inal a part of the park's restroom accommodations.[9] Indeed, several companies had designed, manufactured, and marketed similar products as early as the 1930s,[10] yet despite nearly a century's worth of innovation, the female urinal just did not make its intended splash.

In this instance, the product seems to have fostered a pretty solid association with one gender, making a version intended for the other a hard sell. What happens, however, when no similar innovation is invented, but the product itself is perceived by consumers to be associated with one gender or the other? That is, what if a product is intended for one gender, but consumers see it as something totally different, associating it with another gender altogether? At the very least, confusion is bound to set in.

In one of the more celebrated theses in sociology, Candace West and Don Zimmerman advance the concept of "doing gender,"[11] a theory of how one's performance in everyday life serves to affirm the naturalness of gender—which is, conversely, a social construction. In other words, although it is common to assume that the categories of gender associated with maleness or femaleness are natural, West and Zimmerman demonstrate how these categories are actually created by the way in which people enact their daily routines:

> We contend that the "doing" of gender is undertaken by women and men whose competence as members of society is hostage to its production. Doing gender involves a complex of socially guided perceptual, interactional, and micropolitical activities that cast particular pursuits as expressions of masculine and feminine "natures." . . . Rather than as a property of individuals, we conceive of gender as an emergent feature of social situations: both as an outcome of and a rationale for various social arrangements and as a means of legitimating one of the most fundamental divisions of society.[12]

Drawing out in great detail the nuances of gender as a social construction, the work of West and Zimmerman provides a viable foundation upon which to examine the ways performances that contradict certain attributes associated with a particular gender generate confusion. This certainly does not mean that contradiction is a bad thing, yet if the goal of a beer company is to make a profit, this profit rests largely on the reception of the product by its intended audience—in the case of Zima, males seeking both an alternative look and an alternative taste in beer.

In the alcoholic beverage industry, harnessing the concept of drinks as either masculine or feminine may look like an easy task, yet one might be surprised how much both advertising and the concessions of consumers work together to create these connections. As discussed earlier, while industry commercials often tout an image of masculinity ranging from humorous ramblings and slapstick performances about beer to the sophistication that accompanies the consumption of the stronger varieties of liquor, the goal is to sell the product as something that will bring consumers a step closer to being more attractive, more likable, or even irresistible to the opposite sex, however heteronormative this may be in the end. As the largest target group for most alcoholic products is men, within the industry women have generally played the secondary and unfortunate role of being objects of desire in advertisements. Through this objectification females have been depicted as (among other things) docile, ignorant, desperate, promiscuous, and willing to please their often-intoxicated male partners.

In addition to the power of advertising, consumers also play a big role in circulating the image of men as drinkers and women as their subservient counterparts. From borrowing one-liners popularized in television advertisements to reenacting the absurdities of inebriation that such commercials playfully advance to sell their products, there's little question that individual behavior can be influenced by such marketing—including, of course, the influence on one's perception *of* and *about* either sex.

Regardless of how well advertising strategies and consumer concessions complement each other, the message about how individuals should receive the product is an entirely different and complicated concern for marketing. Despite Coors's efforts to make Zima fit within the masculine camp of beer-drinking aficionados, in reality the new beverage was largely consumed by females, leading to its gradual decline as a male-oriented alcoholic beverage. Now, I am not suggesting that if a product is consumed more by females than males it will necessarily fail; rather, I am highlighting a case in which the intended target audience of males perceived the image of the product as somehow undermining their own manhood, resulting in the subsequent attraction of a secondary audience of females who may not have commanded the same purchasing power as men. After all, females drink beer, have disposable incomes, and certainly make up a portion of stakeholders for the alcoholic beverage industry, but the gray area between which gender Zima should be associated with was never as clear as the drink itself, and this discrepancy proved to be a greater determining factor than the accumulation of dollars and cents. In the end, and however silly, determining which gender the clear Zima beverage was best associated with generated enough confusion to render it obsolete among beer drinkers.

Despite this, as late as 2014, petitions were in circulation to bring back Zima in all its glory:

> We proud and intrepid Zima drinkers have managed to look past Zima's ill-advised, credibility-killing "Zomething Different" advertising campaign of the early '90s; have resisted switching from Zima to more popular "malternative" beverages like Smirnoff Ice and Mike's Hard Lemonade; have continued to bravely drink Zima in public despite catcalls of "it zucks!" and "tastes like zhit!" from smart-alecky

fellow bar patrons; and have even realized that Zima is an excellent (and much more potent) substitute for tonic water in various cocktail recipes. For our devotion to this oft-unfairly-maligned alcopop beverage, we deserve to be able to continue enjoying its fresh citrus essence and bubbly effervescence.[13]

Perhaps this is one indication that Zima iz ztill zought after by zome.

CHAPTER 13

WOW Chips

Just as every generation has a fitness craze, each fitness craze has its accompanying recommendations for dietary changes: eat less; drink less; eat more of the good stuff and less of the fatty, salty, and sugary stuff. Yet every so often, the science behind food manufacturing offers a bit of relief for those missing their snacking habits. In 1998, they received a crunchy little respite when Frito-Lay went national with its WOW chips containing the nonfat wonder ingredient Olestra. Largely marketed as versions of Doritos, Ruffles, and Tostidos,[1] WOW chips maintained their junk food flavor by using Olestra as a substitute for the fat proscribed by popular healthy dietary standards, creating a chip with no fat, no cholesterol and few to no calories. The name WOW was actually putting it lightly, as the label generated a snacking revolution, doing for the image of the potato chip what some believed saccharin and other alternative sweeteners had done for the soft drink.

Yet by the end of the decade most of the hype had—both figuratively and literally—gone down the toilet; the gastrointestinal side effects associated with Olestra caused painful and uncomfortable bowel movements, with the attendant embarrassment of rushing to restrooms and frequently failing to arrive in time. In contrast with the company's slogan that "No one can eat just one," for those chips containing Olestra, it would seem that Frito-Lay failed to give consumers enough reason to keep coming back for more.

Few epic failures in this book are as clearly and wholly attributable to consumer dissatisfaction as Lay's WOW chips. This product, which had the potential to enable guiltless snacking, simply couldn't pass the rudimentary test of cost-benefit analysis: consuming the chips simply wasn't worth the pain—and potential embarrassment—of digesting them.

Although Olestra turned out to be a flash in the pan, it had rather interesting beginnings. According to Marion Nestle, Olestra was discovered unintentionally in the late 1960s when two Procter & Gamble (P&G) researchers were seeking readily digestible foods for premature infants. Though it is a bit on the technical side, Nestle's explanation of Olestra's origins is worth reading:

> Conventional fats are composed of a "backbone" of a small sugar (glycerol) to which three fatty acids are attached, one to each of *three* linkage sites on the sugar. P&G scientists replaced the glycerol with sucrose (common table sugar) to which up to *eight* fatty acids could be attached. The resulting olestra molecule is so much larger than natural fats that it cannot be broken down either by normal digestive processes in the small intestine or by bacterial digestion in the large intestine. The molecule is too big to be absorbed across the intestinal wall to any appreciable extent; it cannot be metabolized and therefore produces no calories. In addition, P&G scientists were able to manipulate the fatty acid composition of olestra to give it the thickness, cooking properties, and taste of natural fats and oils. Hence it could substitute for any conventional oil to prepare fast foods, restaurant meals, or, for that matter, foods cooked at home.[2]

In layperson's terms, Olestra was every bit a miraculous discovery, especially given its potential to taste so similar to natural fats and oils while delivering none of the drawbacks that contribute to weight gain and unhealthy dieting. And a miracle it may have been, but in the United States even miracles are subject to regulation.

Between the mid 1970s and the early 1980s, initially focusing its attention on a pharmaceutical development for lowering cholesterol, P&G took Olestra to the FDA and petitioned for approval, but without the substantial results in testing needed to satisfy regulators, P&G set Olestra aside. In 1985, however, breakfast giant Kellogg Company began to tout evidence that high-fiber foods like cereal could reduce consumers' risk of developing cancer, and P&G saw an opportunity.

Redirecting its focus away from pharmaceutical development and toward food products, P&G sought to develop Olestra as a food additive. Once again, the FDA raised some red flags, largely concerned that if Olestra were to enhance foods typically thought to be on the unhealthy side of the food spectrum with a harmless additive substitute, consumers might get the wrong idea about what they should be eating and perhaps even begin to frequently overeat foods they assumed were now healthy. According to Nestle, the FDA had some other major concerns, including:

- Olestra causes gastrointestinal problems (pain, gas, diarrhea, leakage) in some people.
- Olestra reduces absorption of fat-soluble vitamins.

Although the simple Lay's potato chips were arguably the first and most popular WOW product, Olestra was also featured in Doritos, Tostitos, and Ruffles. ©iStock/Homiel

- Olestra reduces absorption carotenoids and, presumably, other fat-soluble antioxidants and phytochemicals.
- The effects of reduced absorption of fat-soluble nutrients on disease risks are unknown.
- It is not known whether olestra is effective in inducing weight loss or reducing risk factors for chronic diseases.[3]

After several revisions were implemented, the FDA eventually approved the use of Olestra in 1996, although this approval was conditional upon transparency by manufacturers about the additive's potential side effects: "Procter & Gamble, which makes it, and the Frito-Lay Company, the Pepsico subsidiary that manufacturers and sells the chips, [must] report on any adverse health effects. The potato chip packages were also required to carry a label warning of possible gastrointestinal effects."[4] It was the earlier concern about gastrointestinal problems, however, that would prove disastrous to Olestra's reputation.

In 1998, Frito-Lay took the Olestra product to the national market. One of the product's more ironic commercials—in hindsight, of course—features a father and son drifting slowly down a river on inner tubes, the latter taking in the setting sun while the former enjoys a bag of WOW chips. As the narrator finishes singing the nostalgic praises of childhood characterized by carefree living, the son asks his father, "Dad, how are going to get home?" To which the father responds, "You know, son, you worry too much." But the father might well have worried had he known the potentially uncomfortable situation that might befall him as he lay on the inner tube. The fact is that consuming junk food containing Olestra was anything but a simple, carefree experience. To be sure, there are no exceptions to the rules of the route from consumption to digestion, and what is pleasurable going into the body isn't always as pleasurable on the way out.

Consumers learned this firsthand, but not before being "WOWed" by the possibility of an additive that might remove what is unhealthy about an unhealthily manufactured snack. One early consumer, thrilled that her one guilty pleasure had been reduced to simply a pleasure, commented:

> I love Doritos.
> I have loved them as long as I can remember. I love the telltale orange mess they leave on your fingers and face; I love finding the chip that has so much "nacho cheese" on it that it is almost red; I love the way they taste with a cold diet soda; I'll even be so gauche as to say that I love the unmistakable stench of Doritos breath. . . .
> And then came olestra. When Frito-Lay introduced its WOW line of snacks (now called Lay's Light snacks), made with this new kind of "fat," my taste buds tingled. From what I'd heard, olestra (marketed under the brand name Olean) offered the best of both worlds. Because it is, in fact, a fat, the taste and mouth-feel was virtually the same. But here's the kicker: The fat in olestra in indigestible, thus not absorbable. The fatty molecules are simply too big to be metabolized by enzymes and bacteria in the gut. Hallelujah! I could have my cake and eat it too.
> Needless to say, I jumped on the Olean train with glee, snapping up bags and bags of WOW Doritos. All was well. It was a veritable summer of love. Pretty much every day after work, as I watched the evening news, I camped out on the couch with my (newly) guilt-free treat.[5]

Some testers even began to anticipate the new potential of snacking. Said one individual taste-testing the lesser-known Pringles version: "Tastes like Pringles . . . no fat. . . . I guess I can sit down now and eat half a bag."[6] Later, when asked if she knew about the side effects, the taste-tester snickered: "I have a stomach of steel."[7]

I remember having these WOW chips in our home in the late 1990s. My two sisters and I were in our early twenties, and these new additions to our young and idealistic college lifestyle seemed to complement our healthy dieting and exercise routines. Like the refrigerator full of diet soft drinks, low-fat salad dressing, and zero-calorie this, that, and the other thing, WOW chips rang no alarms for us; rather, we considered them the cat's meow.

Of course, numbers were at least as important as taste, as far as Frito-Lay was concerned. The *New York Times* reported just a year after the beginning of the nationwide marketing campaign, "Frito-Lay, by adding olestra versions of its already popular Doritos, Ruffles, Tostitos and Lay's chips and calling them Wow snacks, pulled in $347 million last year, according to Information Resources Inc. Procter & Gamble's olestra version of Pringles chips added $100 million, the company said."[8]

Profits were certainly profits, but within roughly a year Frito-Lay's profits had fallen to half of those from the previous year. That decline in profits was attributable to one thing: the same gastrointestinal concern addressed earlier by the FDA was looming over the wonder ingredient.

During the taste-testing phase of the WOW chip, the nonprofit Center for Science in the Public Interest (CSPI) led a campaign criticizing Procter & Gamble, Frito-Lay, and other companies for their use of Olestra. Michael Jacobson, executive director of CSPI, remarked that "[s]evere side effects might be acceptable from a cancer drug, but they are completely unacceptable from a food additive consumed by millions of people. Consumers shouldn't have to play Russian roulette with their health when they eat a few potato chips."[9]

Jacobson assembled a team of health experts that would gather substantial evidence about Olestra's side effects, which included "abdominal cramping, diarrhea, fecal incontinence, and other gastrointestinal symptoms."[10] In 1997 Jacobson and CSPI had already collected enough data to begin a rather heated debate about the health concerns posed by Olestra, holding a press conference that shed light on a much more controversial story about impact of the ingredient. In a telling series of testimonies, the CSPI released the following statements:[11]

> A 30-year-old mother of four from Plainfield, Indiana, said that her 14-year-old daughter experienced abdominal cramps after school after eating about 30 Cooler Ranch Wow Doritos at lunch. Her 12-year-old son experienced diarrhea for seven days, and gas after snacking on about 5 ounces of Nacho Cheese Wow Doritos at home. He had an accident in bed at 4 a.m., and missed two days of school.

* * *

> [One woman] said that she, her husband, and two sons—ages eight and four—got sick after eating Barbeque-flavored Wow chips. All four suffered fecal urgency, diarrhea, nausea, flatulence, discolored stools, and abdominal cramps.

* * *

A 71-year-old homemaker from Beech Grove, Indiana, got very sick after eating half of a sample bag of chips—about half an ounce. She experienced nausea, severe abdominal cramps, and vomiting. She ate the Wow chips around 3:00 p.m. as a snack, and the symptoms lasted until 4 the next morning.

* * *

A 63-year-old pet groomer from Indianapolis ate half of a family-sized bag of Lay's original Wow chips (about 6 ounces of chips) as a snack and suffered severe and horrible smelling gas, bloating, flatulence, yellow-orange stains, and greasy stools. The symptoms occurred while she was at work and lasted until 2 a.m. that morning. Her 29-year-old daughter experienced cramps and diarrhea.[12]

Testimonies like this were only the tip of the iceberg, as one journalist found that "more than 18,000 adverse reaction reports were submitted to the FDA."[13] In the end, the initial regulatory concerns of the FDA had merit, yet the rush to market and profit motive moved at a faster clip than concern for the public well-being.

Despite the carefree consumption of the low-calorie chips, critics argued that snacking like this came at a gastronomical price. ©iStock/gpointstudio

To be fair, in considering the demand for products that pacify the critics of endless health movements, Olestra—and by extension, the WOW brand—was more of a messenger of sorts, affirming the "no-pain, no gain" dictum that so often accompanies the latest fitness craze. Though it's typically poor form to kill the messenger, WOW chips simply couldn't withstand the public scrutiny; after the news of Olestra's side effects became public, it was a blemish to one's image to be seen with the WOW chips. Indeed, like the account that follows, online posts criticizing WOW chips are almost always qualified with a statement to the effect that the commenter him- or herself was not actually a victim of the chips' more embarrassing side effects: "Oh, and then there's the horror of all horrors: anal leakage—underwear staining caused by the seepage of liquid olestra through the anal sphincter. Lovely. (For the record, I escaped unscathed—and unsoiled—in that department.)"[14] It seems that the quest for guiltless pleasures sometimes conjures up a sense of guilt by association.

The psychology of self-image aside, it should be noted that notwithstanding the evidence that Olestra *can* cause gastrointenstinal discomfort, it may not always be the only cause. Diarrhea, one of the major side effects associated with Olestra consumption, is rather common, so attributing it solely to Olestra might not be exactly fair or accurate. As Malcolm Gladwell explains,

> Olestra has never won the full acceptance of the nutrition community. Most of this concern, however, appears to be overstated. Procter & Gamble has done randomized, double-blind studies—one of which involved more than three thousand people over six weeks—and found that people eating typical amounts of Olestra-based chips don't have significantly more gastrointestinal problems than people eating normal chips. Diarrhea is such a common problem in America—nearly a third of adults have at least one episode each month—that even F.D.A. regulators now appear to be convinced that in many of the complaints they received Olestra was unfairly blamed for a problem that was probably caused by something else.[15]

In short, things like this can happen, and they can't always be attributed to the potato chips you eat.

The failure of WOW chips, however, wasn't the proverbial "throwing the baby out with the bathwater." Indeed, Olestra has lived on in other chip products branded by Kellogg's Pringles—once a P&G brand—albeit alongside other ingredients and in no way as pronounced as it was in Lay's WOW product line. Oddly enough, Olestra is even found in Lay's Light chips today. And some research has suggested that there are indeed redeeming health benefits from Olestra consumption, namely, the reduction of carcinogens like polychlorinated biphenyls.[16] Olestra has also been more recently used outside of the food industry as a lubricant for power tools and even as paint for outdoor decking. Now there's a "WOW moment"—learning that what was once considered to be an amazing substitute in unhealthy diets was useful for lubricating tool parts and staining decks all along!

CHAPTER 14

Y2K

In 1841 Charles Mackay published *Extraordinary Popular Delusions and the Madness of Crowds*, an incredibly entertaining book about collective human interaction during times of speculation. Mackay documents everything from modern prophecies of the Christian Judgment Day[1] in Great Britain to the Dutch infatuation with tulips known as Tulipomania.[2] Although all these cases are threaded together by the notion of what people do when they collectively ride the wave of speculation, Mackay makes only subtle mention of the lack of credibility these cases held, all but ignoring the phenomenon of failure among them. This chapter takes a closer look at how the social phenomenon of rumor gives rise to the idea of end times, highlighting how the popular delusions leading up to a failed event might take precedence over the actual event itself.

For every narrative explaining the beginning of time, there are dozens more speculative ideas about its end. Indeed, the end of the world has become a subject of fascination for the religious and the secular alike. In the former context, eschatological events dot the timelines of just about every faith-based tradition. Some, like the Jehovah's Witnesses, have racked up dozens of failed prophecies touting the end of the world, experiencing dissonance, reorganizing their prescient claims, and then settling in for yet another prophecy failure. Others simply await the end in much more rational terms, anticipating some event, assured of its arrival through liturgy, but rarely actually going out on a limb to suggest a specific date.

In the latter, more secular context, as recently as 1995 one of the closest nuclear war calls in history unfolded when a Black Brant rocket was nearly mistaken for a US attack on Russia. The rocket, launched by a team of Norwegian and American scientists, was carrying equipment to study weather anomalies. Although this was an actual misunderstanding of intelligence, end times scenarios such as this seem to command a much more serious position in history than those based upon religious commitment.

Along these lines, one item of material culture that keeps us apprised of the potential arrival of the end times is the symbolic Doomsday Clock. Showcasing the volatility of the world's end as dependent upon the shortcomings of international leadership decision-making, the clock is calculated and adjusted by the members of the *Bulletin of Atomic Scientists* at the University of Chicago—something far more intuitive and grounded than speculative reasoning.

Perhaps one of the most publicized secular end-times scenarios was the Y2K scare that unfolded at the turn of the twenty-first century as a result of rumors of an impending disaster associated with a computer malfunction. Dubbed Y2K in reference to the arrival of the year 2000, the potential problem revolved around the expression of years using their last two digits. In the official explanation, the Y2K scare originated due to a decades-old attempt to condense information:

> Since the early days of electronic computing, almost universally, only 2 digits have been used in computer systems to denote the year in date fields. For example, 1998 is denoted as 98. This practice was adopted to save expensive computer memory storage space and programming time. In the 60s and 70s, adding two century digits to a date field would have required storage space probably five times more expensive than that required for two—a cost difficult to justify when the general opinion was that most systems would be obsolete before the end of the century. As a result, in many applications the Year 2000 could be interpreted as 1900 because the computer is unable to distinguish between these years which would both be denoted as 00.[3]

In other words, the change from 1999 (expressed as 99) to 2000 (expressed as 00) had the potential to generate devastating consequences, as computers would be either unable to process calculations or unable to accurately read the data necessary to their daily operations.

As the hype surrounding the millennial changeover increased, people latched onto the idea that computer technology was so vital to everyday life that the situation called for some good old-fashioned collective anxiety. Americans led the charge in ramping up the fear of Y2K; some even capitalized on it by transforming the alarm into items for popular consumption, including hats, T-shirts, posters, and figurines.

Yet the anxiety seemed to go beyond assuaging with the soft relief generated by Y2K memorabilia. In September 1999, for example, information technology research company Gartner Inc. surveyed fourteen thousand individuals about their attitudes toward Y2K. The responses were somewhat alarming: "[Fifty-five] percent of respondents said they plan to withdraw two to six weeks' worth of

The countdown to the year 2000 was fraught with fear and anxiety brought about by a series of zeros. ©iStock/gazanfer

cash from their banks, and 14 percent will withdraw even more. Sixty-five percent intend to modify their stock investments, and 67 percent will be stocking up on more than a week's worth of food."[4]

At the very least, these figures suggest that some people took the threat of the computer glitch very seriously. Moreover, these drastic precautionary actions reaffirmed the reality of the situation, which was that this was not a computer problem but a human one. In other words, humans—not machines—and their fears of losing something they depended so heavily upon, were the real cause for concern; they, in their emotionally fragile state, would ultimately be the real impetus of any catastrophic event that ensued.

Compounded by the rapid rise of internet technology in the late 1990s, the perceived catastrophe was blown enormously out of proportion. Some of the most fervent fear-mongering came from economist Gary North, who warned of major banking disasters leading to rioting and looting. North went on to encourage the purchase of gold bullion, relocation to remote regions of the country, and a general hunkering-down to wait out the storm.

In late 1998, with anxiety mounting, technology historian Edward Tenner explained in much more practical terms what some believed would occur as computers reacted to the turn of the century. With a thread of caution, Tenner noted that

[f]or purposes of payment, a person with a negative age may cease to exist. An elevator or an automobile engine judged by an embedded microprocessor to be overdue for inspection may be shut down. All of our vital technological and social systems are vulnerable to crippling errors. Correcting programs requires time-consuming close inspection by skilled programmers, custom-crafted solutions for virtually every computer system, and arduous testing—and time is running out.[5]

In his extensive *Wilson Quarterly* article exploring the Y2K phenomenon in depth, Tenner mentions the efforts, both civil and governmental, to address the possible outcomes of an actual problem. Yet for the most part, Tenner's piece and others like it seemed to legitimize the potential for a disaster brought about by Y2K.

Not everyone, however, was convinced that Y2K merited such widespread angst. Some campaigns to dispel the Y2K rumors, like the "Facts Not Fiction" leaflet released by the UK government,[6] circulated information for quick reference in an attempt to stem rumors and mitigate anxiety. In the United States, the Clinton administration took the threat seriously enough that it appointed an adviser on the topic, strategizing that one way to repudiate Y2K rumors was to normalize them by highlighting just how often computer systems actually break down—the suggestion being that if computer systems did fail on New Year's Day, why would it be any different than what they do so regularly on other days?[7]

Nonetheless, as the clock struck midnight and the calendar advanced to the year 2000, many of those lying in wait listened in on their transistor radios with some relief, if not disappointment, when the date changed uneventfully. In fact, as the celebration hangovers subsided, reports of actual computer disruptions due to the Y2K problem were few and far between. Furthermore, to the comfort of many Americans, the majority of these disruptions took place outside of the United States. In Japan, for example, at least three Y2K glitches associated with the information communications industry were confirmed, and another three relatively benign incidents pertaining to nuclear-power monitoring systems were inconclusively related.[8] In Australia, ticket validation systems for a few bus lines failed, and in France the screen on a national weather report aired the date as "01/01/19100."[9]

Despite these minor disruptions, the predictions surrounding Y2K were largely failures. It certainly did not materialize on the scale predicted by some pundits, and although it's always nice to be right (even if being right means watching the world fall apart), the failure of Y2K was a good thing. But far more interesting than the failure itself was the buildup of collective uncertainty about Y2K—uncertainty that was driven by rumor.

Sociologists within the subfield of collective behavior have at times made such scares the focus of their studies. Stanley Cohen was one of the first to develop the concept of collective behavior through his work on moral panics, or instances of mass hysteria.[10] Instances of such mass mobilization vary broadly, as the following definition of collective behavior suggests: "Behavior that is relatively spontaneous, volatile, evanescent, emergent, extra-institutional, and short-lived; it emerges or operates in situations in which there are no, or few adequate, clear cut definitions as to what to do from mainstream culture."[11] Unlike more conventional behavior, collective behavior emerges along the margins of everyday occurrences. Although instances of this sort of behavior may include riots, moral panics, spontaneous crowd formation, and the like, as the Y2K scare was largely a rumor-based event, rumor within this theoretical framework provides an important departure for understanding Y2K as a socially significant phenomenon.

The sociologist Tomatsu Shibutani spent much of his career studying rumor, referring to it as merely "improvised news" in which individuals combine their fragmented knowledge of a vague situation and try to make sense of it. According to Shibutani, rumor can be defined as a "recurrent form of communication through which men caught together in an ambiguous situation attempt to construct a meaningful interpretation of it by pooling their intellectual recourses."[12] In this definition, rumor appears to run in contrast to the irrationalities of spontaneous collective behavior, as Shibutani's interpretation conjures up a much more rational process of individuals attempting to solve a problem.

In a recent example of this, in the shell-shocked aftermath of 9/11, there appeared to be a thin line between knowing what was actually going on within this new War on Terror versus speculating about it through amateur fact-finding. In the lead-up to the US invasion of Iraq in 2003, rumors about just how dangerous and powerful Saddam Hussein's arsenal really was became the topic of much debate. Perhaps no other individual fanned the flames of rumor more aggressively than Judith Miller, then Washington Bureau correspondent for the *New York Times*. On September 8, 2002, the *Times* ran a front-page article written by Miller and Michael Gordon that alluded to Iraq's solicitation of "aluminum tubes . . . intended [for] components of centrifuges to enrich uranium."[13] The piece provided just enough trivial information about the threat of weapons of mass destruction to allow the Bush administration to conjure up support for a war. The same morning the article ran, Vice President Dick Cheney referenced the story during his interview with *Meet the Press* host Tim Russert. Cheney commented,

> There's a story in the *New York Times* this morning. . . . It's now public that, in fact, he [Hussein] has been seeking to acquire, and we have been able to intercept and prevent him from acquiring, through this particular channel, the kinds of tubes that are necessary to build a centrifuge. And the centrifuge is required to take low-grade uranium and enhance it into highly enriched uranium, which is what you have to have in order to build a bomb.[14]

As the world watched closely, a number of Bush administration officials, including several cabinet members, made the rounds on the television talk show circuit, echoing the Miller-Gordon article. Yet after more than 100,000 deaths (including both civilians and combatants), no traces of weapons of mass destruction were ever uncovered. It turned out that the main rumor in support of war proved to be false.

Although this sort of collective improvisation in an attempt to understand that which couldn't be understood otherwise may serve a social function, it is important to note that rumors like this can have serious consequences. The proliferation of rumors can magnify confusion, just as unreliable reports at times of crucial decision-making can have severe consequences, such as the impact of the Miller-Gordon article.

In a much more detailed explanation of rumors, Ralph L. Rosnow identifies four variable factors that drive rumors in an economy of speculative reasoning: "general uncertainty,"[15] "outcome-relevant involvement,"[16] "personal anxiety,"[17] and "credulity."[18] As the presence of these four variables increases, the likelihood that rumors will proliferate also increases; conversely, when the presence of these variables decreases, the circulation of the rumors becomes far less likely.

General uncertainty, the first of the four variables, is perhaps most apparent to audiences, yet the functional angle through which rumors are exacerbated is a bit more complex. As Rosnow explains, "[R]umors flourish in an atmosphere of uncertainty because they attempt to relieve the tension of cognitive unclarity."[19] In other words, rumors are like simple human mechanisms that are created to help people make sense of situations in which meaning is not so obvious. Today, years after the turn of the twenty-first century, explanations about the potential for disaster in the Y2K problem are pretty simplistic in both technical and laymen terms, yet these ex post facto explanations cannot re-create the pre-Y2K environmental factors that engendered this uncertainty, including the new and rapidly advancing computer technology of the late 1990s, the understanding of computer processors that was exclusive to students of the information technology disciplines on the rise during that period, and the host of anxieties—religious and secular—associated with the changing century.

In hindsight, the precautionary reaction to Y2K may appear to have been an overreaction, yet in the moment, with frightening rumors about what might take place and without any sort of foreknowledge about what was to come, it's no wonder that the failure of Y2K is such a well-publicized and laughable nonevent event—failing to materialize, and, more embarrassingly, failing to award any respect for those who took the threat so seriously.

Taking a threat seriously is, in and of itself, what seems to personalize and give life to a rumor. It follows that the second variable of rumor formation—one's outcome-relevant involvement, or how important the rumor is to the audience that encounters it—is a vital lifeline for rumor circulation. Of course, computer wonks of the late 1990s must have viewed Y2K as an awfully interesting topic for discussion. I can imagine the end-of-the-year Geek Squad corporate

The hysteria regarding Y2K was exploited by Hollywood with at least one B film produced in 1999: *Y2K* (aka *Terminal Countdown*), starring Academy Award winner Louis Gossett Jr. *Ascot Video/Photofest © Ascot Video*

party looping the audio of Prince's hit song "1999" and intermittently pausing to chat, compare notes, and laugh boisterously about what incredible profits the Y2K scare would bring to their business in the new year. In all fairness, however, those who knew computers well weren't the only individuals who thought Y2K was an important matter, but with so little technical understanding of how it might unfold and limited recourses for trying to prevent it at an individual level, most Americans could do little more than nervously await its arrival and hope for the best.

Rosnow's third variable, personal anxiety, is defined as "an affective state—acute or chronic—that is produced by, or associated with, apprehension about an impending potentially disappointing outcome."[20] The restlessness Y2K generated was extensive personal anxiety, mostly played out in terms of how individuals would be able function without the collective services or personal amenities that had come to characterize the industrialized world. The Federal Aviation Administration, for example, lamented the reality that it would not be possible to fix the glitch by 2000,[21] a rather frightening prospect for holiday travelers. Finances—always a personal concern—were also threatened by Y2K, as individuals were distraught over the prospect of failing ATM technology and miscalculations to their account balances.[22] Even real estate attorneys—of all people—expressed concerns about everything from affected elevators and smoke alarms to heating and air-conditioning units,[23] all of which play a major role in an individual's personal sense of comfort and security.

Finally, Rosnow's fourth variable—credulity—refers to one's belief in the rumor in the absence of adequate evidence in support of it.[24] During the Y2K scare, there was an enormous variation in credulity, ranging from indifference to all-out panic. In terms of credulity, for those who exhibit strong beliefs in a given rumor, Rosnow notes that at least two distinct nuances change the makeup of the rumor: (1) wishful credulity and (2) dreadful credulity.

Wishful credulity includes those instances where individuals attempt to profit from a rumor, perhaps a rumored tip that may lead to a winning bet. On the surface, aside from those who served to gain consulting employment, damage control maintenance positions, or simply the excitement of observing technological breakdowns, there appears to have been very little wishful credulity invested in Y2K rumors. Surprisingly enough, however, one segment of the population had a positive view of an impending disaster: the minority of American premillennialist Christians.

In her longitudinal study of millennialist Christians and belief in Y2K, Andrea Hoplight Tapia documents how some individuals drew upon networks of religious and political ideas that both accommodated the Y2K rumor and advanced it as part of their overall agenda. The responses from Tapia's in-depth interviews demonstrate that for these Christians, Y2K was merely an indication that end times were approaching, and any catastrophe that may ensue would actually pose an important opportunity for Christians to proselytize. According to one of her respondents, the notion of opportunity could not be more apparent:

> Christians should see Y2K as an opportunity. The Elders of my church spend a lot of time and effort talking about the Y2K problem and its opportunities for Christians. Y2K is a call for national repentance. It is an opportunity offered by God before or during the great tribulation to repent and come to God. I'm mostly hopeful now. If people are in need emotionally and physically it would be a great opportunity for ministry.[25]

This shouldn't be misunderstood as Christians looking forward to the misfortune of others, but instead as their interpretation of both an opportunity to spread their teachings and, more importantly, an indication of a well-anticipated event that would reaffirm their belief system. In this way, this group of Americans viewed the potential success of Y2K in a positive light.

In contrast to wishful credulity, individuals viewing the rumor with dreadful credulity held Y2K in a much more negative light. According to Rosnow,

"Dread rumors are those that invoke feared or disappointing consequences. Such rumors in general population seem especially deadly because they can emerge like hobgoblins to spook people into believing the most horrific claims."[26] Perhaps it's safe to assume that most Americans who encountered the rumor and gave any thought to the prospect of a catastrophe generated by Y2K were invested in this form of credulity. The Y2K scare as a secular rumor largely featured this type of dread, yet Tapia's religious sample doesn't seem to account for much of this fearfulness. Surprisingly enough, in contrast to several other responses, the following is much more steeped in dreadful credulity:

> The rapture will happen after the tribulation begins but before God pours out his wrath . . . I know that no man can know the hour of Jesus' return, but the better one knows the Bible the more prepared he or she will be when the time comes. Y2K may be a part of the larger plan to move us closer to endtimes.[27]

The variation of beliefs found in these religious contexts is complex, but institutions that centralize beliefs as such may be a tad bit more susceptible to these rumors. I am certainly not suggesting that level of naïveté is particularly high among the religious; however, most religions, especially those of the salvific sort, typically foster a certain amount of faith that complements strong credulity. In this way, suspending precepts of reality in order to accommodate a commitment to one's faith may limit the critical thought involved in analyzing a rumor's truth claims.

The Y2K scare was a relatively short-lived example of collective behavior based upon little more than rumor. As the presence of the four variables—general uncertainty, outcome-relevant involvement, personal anxiety, and credulity—increased, the Y2K scare followed suit. Although the origins of the rumor contained some factual reasoning, strategies about how to deal with its fallout were well managed and rather promising—so much so that rumors of an ensuing catastrophe probably should have been ignored. Yet, as social scientists have demonstrated so clearly, "rumor tends to fly thick and fast when topical importance is maximized."[28] In this case, the millennial shift from the twentieth to the twenty-first century effectively aggrandized its significance, and although some were certainly anticipating disastrous outcomes—some wishfully, some dreadfully—the entire scare failed to transpire. In the end it was not computer malfunctions, but good old human behavior bound to fear and anxiety that caused the most consternation. As a failed pop-cultural event, the Y2K scare is a true case study in how mass speculation leading up to a well-publicized occasion can take primacy over the very event that generated the speculation. Ultimately, for those of us who depend on computer technology for our everyday needs, this may be one of the more important failures of our time.

CHAPTER 15

XFL

In 2001, just days after the National Football League (NFL) aired its wildly popular annual Super Bowl event, a new football league named the XFL debuted featuring amateur athletes, a host of new rules, and an edgy hypermasculine spin. An odd curiosity that generated some initial interest, the XFL played out a three-month season, after which it folded in what has come to be known as one of the most incredible failures in organized sports. Not to go too far down the path of superstition, it is worth noting that this failure may have arrived in the company of at least one bad omen: on January 30, 2001, a blimp advertising the XFL's debut flew out of control over Oakland, California, eventually crashing into the Oyster Reef restaurant along the Oakland waterfront.[1] In a similar trajectory to that of the blimp, the XFL quickly ascended to popularity before abruptly falling into failure.

At first glance, what is bizarre about this case is that unlike other popular failures discussed in this book, the XFL wasn't a strange adaptation of a hamburger, a poorly produced movie, or even a lip-syncing nightmare, but rather a version of the highly popular sport of football—the very epitome of *Americana*. So how did something that so embodies the culture of American sports become such an enormous failure? Everyone had a theory. Some believed that the biggest problem was the timing of the XFL's season; running from February to April, it was forced to compete with the National Basketball Association as it turned toward playoff season as well as the college basketball tradition of March Madness that annually takes over the world of televised sports.

Others, like the great sports commentator Bob Costas, argued that the airing of games during prime time in the evenings—as opposed to on the weekends, as was traditional—contributed to league's demise. According to Costas,

Another part of the problem, I think, was that it was in prime time. Had it been in the normal weekend sports slots, that's one thing, but these were getting record low prime time ratings, and also drawing the attention of not just the sports writers, but of the variety types, the Hollywood reporter types, because it's entertainment programming.[2]

These issues may have helped to craft the league's coffin, but there were certainly other factors involved in the XFL's decline.

Practically speaking, there were some rather pronounced differences between the rules of football in the XFL and those of the NFL, which presented a steep learning curve challenge for fans of the NFL. The game opened with an "opening scramble" in place of the traditional coin toss, which was more of a footrace between two players from the 30-yard line to the 50-yard line in an attempt to gain possession of the football. The XFL had no point-after-touchdown kicks and no fair catches, did not allow forward motion for an offensive linemen positioned outside the tackles, and, for a time at the beginning of the season, had no penalties for full bump-and-run coverage. There were also some logistical differences, including a play clock set five seconds shorter than the NFL's forty-second clock, tie-breakers similar to the NCAA rules, and no unsportsman-like conduct penalties for the celebrations that so often accompany hard hits and touchdowns.

In addition to these differences in rules, the way the game was called and the way audiences experienced game play were also quite different from the NFL. Although there was some professional play-by-play and analysis, most of the coverage was executed by comparatively amateur announcers or former World Wrestling Entertainment (WWE) personalities like Jesse Ventura, Jim Ross, and Jerry Lawler. But if the game was lacking in professional coverage and analysis, it was certainly not short of an inside view of commentary by the players and coaches commentary, as there was a pointed effort to capture all the testosterone-laden trash talk: In addition to the on-field cameramen who documented the hard-hitting action, coaches and players had microphones attached to their uniforms, offering the audience a taste of what it sounds like within scrimmage. However, this feature, clever as may have been, was not enough to guarantee the XFL's success.

Perhaps the most popular theory of the XFL's demise had little to do with the game itself; instead it was associated with the curious innovations of the league's production that were directly linked to its founder, Vince McMahon Jr., and his involvement with the WWE (formerly known as the World Wrestling Federation). Having cut his teeth in the salacious and ultramasculine world of choreographed wrestling, McMahon sought to bring elements of that world to football and somehow create a fan following for the new league. What this really came down to was ensuring there was the right blend of aggressive male athleticism and female objectification. Of this venture, McMahon commented, "I thought that there was the right complement of sexuality and a right complement of confrontation; the right complement of really good, hard-hitting football."[3] In the mind of McMahon, sexuality, confrontation, and football may have *complemented* each other, but how they were presented wasn't exactly *complimentary* to any of them individually. Rather, the XFL appeared to push sexism instead of sexuality (never mind that neither is necessary in organized sports), failed to distinguish between what it means to engage in sportsmanlike confrontation and simply confrontation, and—though there may have been football present, and with all due respect to the players who participated—it was amateur at best, and certainly not professional.

Nonetheless, McMahon felt the formula for success he had found in turning wrestling from a sport into a form of entertainment could also be applied to football. I don't believe, as some have charged, that McMahon sought to choreograph the game play as he had done in the wrestling ring, but the atmosphere surrounding these games so closely resembled his WWE events that it really was

Vince McMahon Jr., founder of the XFL.
USA Network/Photofest © USA Network

hard to dismiss his presence and influence—which, while highly innovative, was not necessarily the kind of innovation that would create something competitive with the NFL and its success. McMahon and his innovation were thus, in my opinion, major contributors to the XFL's failure.

To better understand how one's presence and innovation might hinder the advances of a given venture, a sociological interpretation may be useful. In sociology, the world of human interaction can be thought of in terms of the interplay between *agency* and *structure*. Where the former refers to an individual's means of determining his or her own experience, the latter is generally used to describe the multiple other individuals and institutions involved in how one perceives a given experience. Although it may seem counterintuitive, the majority of the failures explored in this book are often thought of as flaws among agency, yet they have actually been the result of some form of structural discernment; that is, where consumers tend to blame the individual for the failure of a product or production, there seems to be a kind of collective or even institutional criticism that holds more potential power to define what is labeled a failure. I don't mean to suggest that structural causes are the only reason for failure, as both agency and structure certainly play a role; however, it does seem that in some cases the role of structure is often more telling than the role of individual agency. Given what appears to be a slight imbalance between what accounts for failure, I'd like to give a bit more emphasis to agency in this case. If we set aside how failure occurs in relation to the structure involved in determining it as such, we're left with the producers of the XFL itself—namely, the founder, Vince McMahon.

A self-proclaimed entrepreneur, McMahon followed in the footsteps of his father, Vincent Sr., who made his career as the famed promoter of the Capitol Wrestling Corporation. The younger McMahon took his father's business and transformed the old-fashioned sport into ultramasculine theater in which men exercised their bravado, reaffirming their dominance over and exploitation of women. In a society rife with patriarchy and sexism, McMahon's version of wrestling struck a chord with young and impressionable male audiences, launching his productions to unheard-of success. As of late 2010, two of the WWE's most popular shows, *Smackdown* and *Monday Night Raw*, drew as many as 3.5 and 5 million viewers, respectively, each week.[4] Although McMahon seemed to have tapped into a large demographic of males between the ages of eighteen and thirty-four, he had done so by capitalizing on male insecurities about toughness and needing to control the opposite sex—all bound to heteronormative notions of manhood—through staged encounters between men pushing their athletic limits in close quarters.

This model, however, simply couldn't be imposed upon the type of sport the National Football League had established. This, of course, is not to say that the explotation of similar insecurities has no place in the NFL—there is certainly enough evidence to suggest it does—but the blatant encouragement of this culture of aggression and often lewd and lascivious treatment of women is not a mainstay of the NFL, or of any other major organized sport, for that matter.

With the XFL, McMahon was taking an innovative shot at success—risky, yes, but still quite innovative. Although innovation is often thought of as a positive thing, certainly something akin to creative use of knowledge and ability, it does not always result in accolades. In fact, it is within the "I think I'm going to try something new" moment that perhaps the seeds of failure are sewn.

The sociologist Robert K. Merton contributed to a developing theory known as *structural strain*, in which sociologists explore how the perception of deviant behavior is associated with the disjunction between goals made up of normative values and the acceptable means of achieving them. For Merton, these goals and acceptable means constitute an important, if not determining, factor in how individuals find themselves either inside or outside a given social setting. According to Merton, these goals "consist of purposes and interests, held out as legitimate objectives for all," adding that "they are the things 'worth striving for.'"[5] Of the means, Merton writes: "[E]very social group invariably couples its cultural objectives with regulations, rooted in the mores or institutions of allowable procedures for moving toward these objectives."[6] When the continuity of these ends and the means for obtaining them breaks down, a failure in achieving acceptability occurs. Merton, in advancing this theory, views deviant behavior not necessarily as an inherent quality but instead as the result of a breakdown when one strives for acceptable ends through unacceptable means.

Within this framework, Merton considers how individuals differentially negotiate between these ends and means, identifying five different modes of adaptation: (1) conformity, (2) innovation, (3) ritualism, (4) retreatism, and (5) rebellion. Where *conformity* refers to behavior in which both the ends and the means are agreed upon as acceptable, *innovation* refers to the acceptance of these ends coupled with a rejection of the acceptable means. Conversely, *ritualism* is behavior in which the ends are rejected and the means are accepted—in other words, going through certain motions simply for their own sake; *retreatism* refers to the rejection of both the ends and means, a kind of self-marginalizing behavior that positions one outside of society's normative structure; and, finally, *rebellion* is simply behavior that selectively accepts and/or rejects the ends and/or the means, at times even substituting new ends and new means as the individual sees fit.

Although all the differential outcomes are certainly relevant to a discussion about failure and success, the one mode of adaptation that is particularly relevant to this topic is innovation: seeking to achieve socially agreed-upon ends—in this case, success—through means that challenge the normative behaviors others have traditionally employed. According to Merton,

Great cultural emphasis upon the success-goal invites this mode of adaptation through the use of institutionally proscribed but often effective means of attaining at least a simulacrum of success—wealth and power. This response occurs when the individual has assimilated the cultural emphasis upon the goal without equally internalizing the institutional norms governing ways and means for its attainment.[7]

This line of reasoning suggests that innovation, while something to be admired for the courage involved with taking risks, may nonetheless diminish the acceptability of one's attempts to achieve success.

The application of Merton's reasoning to the XFL is quite simple: McMahon's innovation in the way he went about forming his new league is directly related to the XFL's unfavorable reception by fans and critics. In other words, if we assume for a moment that any start-up league is bent on success as its normative ends, then the main discrepancy between the NFL and XFL is how they went about achieving such ends. At the center of this discrepancy, then, is the NFL's tradition of focusing on athleticism and sportsmanship versus McMahon's attempt to sell sexuality and aggression with a side of football.

Perhaps some of the more obvious innovative ideas pushed by McMahon were those associated with the incorporation of women into the league. Predictably, this didn't materialize in terms of putting females in management or leadership roles, or even soliciting their input about how the league should be developed; instead, women figured into the XFL as marketing gimmicks to be objectified in the presence of a male-dominated audience. Similar to the way he exploited women exploited within his wrestling rings, McMahon made women who were wearing next to nothing a big part of the XFL.

In one tasteless attempt at boosting viewership, for example, the XFL produced and released a commercial narrated by girlish and scantily clad cheerleader Krissy Carlson. Leading a team of geared-up football players, Carlson says: "A lot of you tuned in to the XFL the first week. Unfortunately, most of you never came back. Well, we listened to you and we made the rule changes to give you what you really want. So come back. At halftime, we'll take you into the cheerleaders' locker room."[8]

Indeed, the stunt went off as planned . . . kind of. In an absurd demonstration of poor acting and even poorer taste, the sketch showed the cameraman fantasizing about his trek into the steamy locker room filled with half-naked women preparing for their performance. Why was it only a fantasy? Apparently the cameraman took a fall and knocked himself out, only to be awoken by none other than the angry McMahon himself, kicking and throwing water on the cameraman in the midst of his fainting episode.

Other sexist productions followed suit. In a bizarre ad featuring women dressed in tight XFL halter-top midriffs and black leather hot pants thrusting their hips and gazing vulnerably into the camera, a male narrator launches into a monologue about a fantasy that can somehow be satisfied by the XFL: "The eyes . . . they tell us who she is . . . they tell us she is intelligence. She is strength. She is dignity. She is making me feel like I did when I was a little boy and my mom and dad took me to the circus: there were clowns and monkeys. Daddy wants some popcorn."[9] Like most sexism that flies under the radar of banality, this tricky interference run by a strange regression to the narrator's childhood reveals just how ridiculous the entire commercial—if not the league itself—actually is. If this was the extent to which McMahon was trying to make the changes necessary to bring back an audience, it simply wasn't going to work.

In close relation to the way women were exploited in XFL productions, McMahon saw to it that men had the opportunity to be as "manly" as possible, demonstrating their perceived prowess not only over the opposite sex, but toward their weaker male counterparts as well. Although the majority of this was prepackaged in the lawlessness of many of the rules—or lack thereof—of the game itself, the league's commercial promotions were saturated with hypermasculinity. In one promotional video, for example, McMahon and other producers are featured in a montage of sound bites intended to convey just how tough the XFL was in comparison to the NFL. Most of the chatter in the commercial is about how the NFL was "afraid" to experiment with a different type of football, but it also highlighted McMahon's takeaway—delivered two times, no less—that stated: "This will not be a league for pantywaists or sissies."

McMahon also showcased how boisterous, if not obnoxious, the XFL scene could be by injecting a kind of conflict-baiting over the loudspeaker during games—something that had become a staple in his WWE. To facilitate this model of narrating to the crowd, the XFL frequently embedded the announcers within the audience, creating a much rowdier look because of the face-painted, sign-carrying, and often inebriated fans. In WWE parlance, this is known as "cutting a promo," or executing a skit-like monologue directed toward the fans in which the orator advances a staged feud between himself and another individual. Such monologues typically begin with the orator's grandiose entrance, followed by a virile and vociferous mix of tough-guy chatter about the type of pain and damage he's about to inflict upon his opponent. In something of a crossover between the WWE and the XFL, on one occasion, McMahon featured the popular wrestling personality Dwayne Johnson, known as The Rock, in character and cutting a promo during the introduction of a match between the Chicago Enforcers and the Los Angeles Xtreme. With a cock-of-the-walk attitude in full force, The Rock addresses what appears to be a more than half-empty stadium of fans in Los Angeles, pitching his insults not toward another wrestler but instead the NFL itself. In WWE parlance, his "beef" can be chalked up to the lack of an NFL team in Los Angeles, with praise for the XFL for bringing a professional team to town. In order to better illustrate the type of talk cutting a promo entails, I've included a substantial part of The Rock's diatribe here:

> So we have a little message to the NFL suits: We want you to find your bags—the very bags you packed when you took football out of LA—then we want you to empty your bags out, and then we want you to fill your bags back up with the things that are obviously more important to you. We want the NFL to fill their bags up with their little cell phones . . . with their little dinner reservations . . . and then we want you to add one more thing: a brand new red-and-black XFL football! And once you've added that football, we want you to zip your bags up—make sure they're nice and tight and secure—and then we say to you, the NFL suits, and to everyone around who wants to tell us, the people, what we should have and what we shouldn't have . . . we respectfully tell you to take your bags, turn 'em sideways, and stick them straight up your CANDY ASSES! If you SMELLLLL what the XFL is cooking![10]

Of course, the fans loved this display of manliness and coded homophobia; it was, after all, the type of entertainment this loyal fan base was so used to watching in the WWE.

In addition to objectifying women and showcasing masculinity at every turn, the XFL did feature some football. The league itself was organized into two divisions, Eastern and Western, with four teams in each division. The Eastern Division was made up of the Birmingham Thunderbolts, the Chicago Enforcers, the New York/New Jersey Hitmen, and the Orlando Rage, while the Western Division included the Las Vegas Outlaws, the Los Angeles Xtreme, Memphis Maniax, and the San Francisco Demons. All teams were competing for a chance to play in the Million Dollar Game, the championship game for which the winning team would literally be awarded $1 million, to be divided equally among the winning team's thirty-eight players.

The lead-up to this Million Dollar Game, however, lacked entertainment value. The players, of course, were truly invested in the game, but the caliber of play just couldn't come close to the action-packed competition of even the NFL's in-season play. Although it is difficult to make a fair and accurate comparison between the two leagues, quantitatively or qualitatively, the 2001 season statistics tell at least some of the story. Even accounting for the difference between the number of games played in each league's season—teams in the NFL played sixteen versus the XFL's ten—the offensive numbers paint drastically different pictures: Marshall Faulk of the St. Louis Rams led the NFL with 1,382 total rushing yards, while John Avery of the Chicago Enforcers topped the XFL with 800 total yards. In total touchdowns, Faulk again topped the NFL with twenty-one, compared to eight from Darnell McDonald of the Los Angeles Xtreme. And Kurt Warner of the St. Louis Rams held the title that year for most yards passing, with 4,830, versus 2,186 yards from Los Angeles Xtreme's Tommy Maddox.

The defensive numbers painted a similar picture, but again these comparisons merely scratch the surface, as the overall athletic abilities of the players were, frankly, as different as night and day. Costas weighed in on the topic, quipping: "It has to be at least a decade since I first mused out loud, 'Why doesn't somebody combine mediocre high school football with a tawdry strip club?' Finally, somebody takes my idea and runs with it."[11] Costas's remarks, however cynical, were rather accurate, and after the first week of play, the fans certainly seemed to notice.

Still recovering from the hangover driven by some taste of success—the first week of play drew a 9.5 Nielsen rating—during the second week of XFL play, McMahan watched his new league take a nosedive. Their initial curiosity spent, fans simply didn't come back to watch on television, much less to the live games. After some pathetic attempts to lure a fan base through racy marketing and loud but empty banter about how the league was coming of age, the league limped painfully through rest of the season, with criticism after criticism pilling up on its breaking back.

Characterizing the whole frustrating ordeal, in March 2001 McMahon lost what little cool he had left during a rather heated interview with Costas for the HBO Sports program *On the Record with Bob Costas*. During what seemed to be the last breath of commercial air in the XFL's short life, McMahon defended the league by reiterating over and over again that creating a new league was a difficult process, and that where time had been on the side of the NFL in capturing acclaim, most critics were prematurely adjudicating the quality of the XFL without considering just how challenging it is to sell something so new. Noticeably displeased with Costas's no-nonsense style of inquiry, McMahon came off as defensive and at one point even intimidating toward his interviewer. In what amounted to one uncomfortable and unprofessional rant after another, the episode clearly showed that both McMahon and his league had lost what little respect and interest the mainstream sports community had graciously granted them—and that would ever be reinstated.

At the close of the inaugural season, McMahon packed up his league and went back to the world of wrestling. His attempt at crafting a new kind of football outside the boundaries of the establishment NFL had gone kaput. When asked by Costas how much money he had lost on the league, McMahon declined to say, but he did acknowledge that it was in the "tens of millions"[12]—perhaps a drop in the bucket in terms of the wealth McMahon has acquired over the years, but the resulting stigma may have been the real cost. In spite of it all, Mc-

Mahon's brand of wrestling, with added raunchy flavor, still captures millions of viewers every week—a success in a market where that kind of entertainment is still appealing. Yet if McMahon were ever again to try to replicate that appeal in another established sport, I would bet on not only another epic fail, but a real disconnect between what it means to learn from one's costly ends as lessons and the lessons that one can learn from its costly means—whatever level of innovation such lessons may present.

CHAPTER 16

McAfrika

In friendly communication, mixing day-to-day talk with contentious topics can really make for an awkward conversation—especially when it comes to politics and food. In 2003, for example, United States representatives Robert W. Ney and Walter B. Jones demonstrated their disfavor for France's opposition to the US invasion of Iraq by advocating that cafeterias in the House office buildings replace French fries with "freedom fries" and French toast with "freedom toast."[1] If the French were not already aware of some of our leadership's discontent with their government for not prematurely arriving at conclusions that would lead them to war, from that point both the congressional minutes and the cafeteria menus reflected that freedom, not the French, was our real ally.

This example of political posturing bound to bizarre strands of nationalism is not the only time in history when food and politics collided. In 2002, at the height of several devastating famines caused by war and drought in Africa, McDonald's introduced the McAfrika hamburger in Norway. With McDonald's franchises dotting the landscape all over the industrialized world and beyond, a pita bread, beef patty, lettuce, and tomato concoction may not have seemed too far out of the ordinary if not for its rather uncanny name, referencing the poorest continent on earth. Why not, for example, name it the McEurope, which certainly would have jibed better with the geographic location of Norway? McDonald's could have even worked upon rugged and robust stereotypes and named it the McAustralia or even the McOutback. McAntarctica would have been a relatively neutral, albeit cold, reference. Or maybe the McNorth (or -South) America would have been a fitting name—after all, why not give tribute to the original home of the beefy hamburger world, where trees are leveled to make way for grazing? Despite the plethora of options, however, this new menu item was said to actually have the taste of Africa, so why wouldn't McDonald's call it McAfrika?[2]

As one of the wealthiest nations on earth, Norway was a rather bizarre place to begin marketing a hamburger that would conjure up such a crisis of semantics, risking the company's image and thrusting it into the world of politics. Yet shortly after crowds of conscientious Norwegians—who had made the link between profiteering and the then-current tragedy of famine—began protesting the new hamburger, McDonald's did something unexpected—by doing nothing at all. Rather than pulling the hamburger from the menu and making an immediate apology, McDonald's tiptoed around the marketing disaster by issuing a nonapology apology that only really addressed the company's poor timing. As one *Guardian* journalist reported, "Margaret Brusletto, a spokeswoman for the company, said she was sorry the name of the product had offended many. 'That wasn't our intention [and] we acknowledge that we have chosen an unfortunate time to launch this new product.'"3 McDonald's eventually negotiated an informal compromise by allowing aid agencies the opportunity to leave donation boxes and post antifamine literature in its Norwegian restaurants, yet during its promotional run the McAfrika remained a part of the company's fast-food menu.4

The McAfrika was not the first major failure in McDonald's history. In fact, a series of menu mistakes preceded it, including but not limited to the 1963 Hulaburger, a pineapple-slice-based creation designed to accommodate Catholic customers during Lent; the 1987 McPizza, which failed to compete in the fast-food pizza boom of the late 1980s; the 1993 McLobster that was overpriced compared to the other McDonald's menu items and had an awfully unappealing appearance; and even the 2006 McRib, which, unlike most rib meals, was served boneless. Perhaps the biggest experimental failure was the 1996 Arch Deluxe, a relatively simple burger that broke the model of a fast-food item and targeted a more sophisticated clientele.5 But unlike the Arch Deluxe and other related menu failures, the McAfrika entered a politicized sphere by commercially evoking the name of a continent that had historically been subject to injustice, exploitation, and recurring famine. As one senior policy adviser at Norwegian Church Aid put it, "Twelve million people are suffering from starvation in countries such as Malawi and Zimbabwe; it is one of the biggest humanitarian disasters we have ever seen. We have nothing against McDonald's but the timing of this is insensitive."6 The glaring irony of the situation was that the abundance of food in the developed world was being paraded around in the form of menu item supposedly originating from a region that was experiencing severe shortages in consumable goods—not the least of which was food.

As if the commercial disaster that was the McAfrika was not enough for one decade, McDonald's decided to add to the mess by introducing a menu item with almost the same name a mere six years later, introducing a slightly different sandwich called the McAfrica in the United States. Marketed as a promotional hamburger during the 2008 Olympics, advertisements claimed this new McAfrica was "a taste of Africa with two all-beef patties, cheese, fresh tomato, and lettuce dressed with an exotic African sauce of mayonnaise and spices."[7] Eight years into the twenty-first century, McDonald's might have exercised a tad more cultural sensitivity by excluding the "exotic" reference, but that the company demonstrated no restraint when it came to making the same political mistake twice was the real impetus for the failure—again—of the menu item.

How was the incorporation of such a reference so detrimental to the success of something as inconsequential as a fast-food menu item? The answer, though complex, lies in the symbolism engendered by the references themselves. The work of twentieth-century French cultural theorist Roland Barthes is particularly useful for interpreting the milieu of this food item controversy. Known largely for his application of structural analysis to popular culture, Barthes viewed all cultural phenomena as signs embedded within a larger system of relational structures—namely, structures of language. This analysis, then, is the basis for his interpretation of semiology: "Semiology—aims to take in any situation of signs, whatever their substance and limits; images, gestures, musical sounds, objects, and the complex associations of all these, which form the content of ritual, convention or public entertainment; these constitute, if not languages, at least systems of signification."[8] Thus nonlinguistic sign systems ranging from fashion

Unlike this 2012 Hamburger Royal TS from a German McDonalds, the McAfrika drew criticism for its cultural insensitivity. ©iStock/PeJo29

and architecture to automobiles and food may be viewed as items that can be interpreted through structural analysis.

In his 1957 treatise on material culture titled *Mythologies*, Barthes attempts to demythologize modern myths—what he views as *ideology*—by exposing the underlying messages associated with certain dominant values, namely, those of the bourgeois class. Along this line of reasoning, Barthes teases out the tenuous connections between objects, their perceived identities, and their meanings. In France, for example, one aspect of the national identity that developed along with the nation-state is the culture of consuming wine. According to Barthes, products such as cheese and wine are uniquely characteristic of France. Of course, this does not suggest that these products originated in France or that they are exclusive to French cuisine, but rather supports the mythological notion that there is something innately French about them. Barthes reasons that wine in particular has a mythological association with France in the same way milk is the "totem drink" of the Dutch, or tea that of the British.[9] In this way, the material culture itself has a certain quality about it that has come to generate an association between a nation and its citizens—an example of mythmaking.

This mythology, as Barthes refers to it, was not merely a symbolic phenomenon but also one that produced differences in perception about how to interact with the material culture itself. In fact, Barthes adds that non-Frenchmen drink for pleasure and the intention of getting drunk, whereas Frenchmen get drunk only as a consequence, never intentionally. Thus, the myth of this symbolic material permeates our sense of reality and even provides us with information about how national borders can separate different types of people with different types of motivations and intentions, regardless of how fuzzy the logic may be in actuality.

Building upon this thesis, Barthes goes on to develop an instructive distinction between an obvious meaning and that which might be considered nothing more than subtext. In other words, on the surface, any item has a literal (denotative) meaning, yet the socially constructed (connotative) meaning is less apparent, and that is what Barthes sets out to reveal. For example, toys are largely seen as playthings intended to occupy children's imaginations; however, this is merely a descriptive meaning apparent to most audiences. Yet toys, in at least one other social function, serve to convey certain prescriptions within a society. In the following example, the connotative significance of socially constructed gender roles is subtly embodied with the material culture itself: "There exist, for instance, dolls which urinate; they have an oesophagus, one gives them a bottle, they wet their nappies; soon, no doubt, milk will turn to water in their stomachs. This is meant to prepare the little girl for the causality of house-keeping, to 'condition' her to her future role as mother."[10] These items and their less apparent meanings complicate the world of material culture to the extent that all items are actually part of an intricate structure of signs and systems of significance.

In accordance with the nomenclature of structural analysis, Barthes interprets these signs as having multiple meanings, beginning foremost with the fundamental relationship between *signifier* (an object, image, sound, etc.) and *signified* (its message, concept, meaning, etc.). In other words, all signs are constructed through a relationship between their signifier and signified parts; these relationships are solidified through an exchange within a larger structure of difference in which cultural codes adhere to various combinations.

For the McAfrika and the subsequent McAfrica, the names may be seen as signs composed of their signifiers (the actual visual combination of letters that comprise a word), and their signifieds (the conceptual ideas of the continent of Africa as a sociocultural representation with an actual history). This relationship, however, reveals only the name's denotative meaning, or its particularly obvious meaning in relation to the intentions of both the marketer who labeled it as such as well as the people who encounter it. For Barthes, however, unlike this denotative meaning, it is the connotative meaning that generates a much more complex and meaningful significance.

As all cultural phenomena are susceptible to the influence of a dominant class, the analytical model of sign, signifier, and signified is open to further meanings that permeate beyond the denotative. These new signs occur when the original sign becomes yet another signifier altogether. Barthes refers to these secondary meanings in combination with each other as *sign-functions*, effectively combining the denotative and the connotative.[11] For these McDonald's menu item creations, new signifiers embedded in the original sign become objects representing a subtle continuity of exploits from the past and the compounded tragedies of famine that this exploitation played such a strong role in creating.

Take, for example, a somewhat controversial advertisement from the clothing and accessory company Benetton depicting a black woman nursing a white baby. Using his famous marketing strategy of replacing the product with sociopolitical—often litigious—images, Benetton photographer Oliviero Toscani may have been conveying any number of critical messages with this image; yet if his intended message had anything to do with racial harmony, the reception of that message may have been a difficult sell due to the dynamics of the symbolism involved. As Marita Sturken and Lisa Cartwright explain,

> The image can be understood in the history of images of mother and child, although its meaning is contingent on the viewer's assumption, on the basis of the contrast of their skin color, that this woman is not

the child's biological mother but its caretaker. While in certain contexts, this image might connote racial harmony, in the United States it carried other connotations, most troubling the history of slavery in the United States and the use of black women slaves as "wet nurses" to breast-feed the white children of their owners. Thus, the intended meaning of this image as an icon of an idealized interracial mother-child relationship is not easily conveyed in context where image's meanings are *overdetermined* by historical factors.[12]

The multiple meanings surrounding this image are thus bound to a network of significations, few of which are passively interpreted as simply a woman feeding a baby. Yet, surprisingly enough, these passive interpretations are precisely the types of understanding that allow for an image like this to circulate without the slightest reference to how it may be deconstructed through critical analysis—not to mention, of course, the tendency of consumers to passively consume without regard for the consequences of their purchases.

However, with enough signification in circulation that makes reference to this contentious relationship between the image and history, the signifiers therein become overdetermined. It is this overdeterminism of signifiers, mentioned by Sturken and Cartwright, that seemingly permits the image to be cast in relative banality. As the cultural critic Henry A. Giroux notes about the Benetton ad, this overdeterminism may be viewed as twofold:

> First, the racial coding of the image is so overdetermined that it is difficult to imagine that this black women nursing a long, pale pink baby is the child's mother. Given the legacy of colonialism and racism that informs this image, I also believe that the photo privileges a range of dominant readings that suggest the ingrained racial stereotype of the black/slave/wet nurse or mammy. Other than the logo, there are no signifiers in this photo which would threaten or rupture such an imperialist coding. It is precisely the absence of referents of resistance, rupture, and critique that allows the reader to be perfectly comfortable with such a configuration of race and class while at the same time accepting the image as nothing more than a "playful" ad.[13]

With the Benetton example in mind, the sign-function of the McDonald's menu items may be seen in a much more different light, well beyond the denotative meaning as a mere item of consumption.

Analysis such as this requires that one take note of what is being viewed and the meanings that can be derive from it. Objects in general may be viewed irrespective of their denotative meaning, without explicitly stating that they have been viewed as such. This, after all, is what took place to some extent when some apologists from the organization African Youth in Norway welcomed the McAfrika, arguing that there had been too much bad publicity about Africa in the media and that this new menu item might actually be a positive thing. As one spokesman commented:

> The word Africa does not need to be associated with war, hunger, AIDS and catastrophes all the time. Finally we see someone who uses the continent's name in a positive way. Even though there is a terrible shortage of food in some areas of Africa, this is far from the situation all over the continent. I really resent the aid organisations painting a picture of a continent full of hunger and despair.[14]

But for those who were sympathetic to the broader call for help from a place in world where starvation echoed loudly, the label just appeared insensitive. The very combination of the profit-seeking corporation's ubiquitous prefix "Mc" and the reference to the continent of Africa, which has become a locus of real-life tragedies, seemed to be yet another insult.

On the surface, the variations of breads, meats, vegetables, and sauces bound to some commercially contrived name seem relatively harmless. Yet fast-food companies that possess such incredible market shares should arguably exercise a modicum of responsibility if they want to retain their positions in the industry. Unfortunately, this type of responsibility is not always an objective.

For the two McDonald's menu items that will go down in history as failures for disregarding such objectives, very little was actually at stake. In the end, McDonald's is so widely successful that minor failures—even controversial ones like the McAfrika and McAfrica—may be better viewed as convenient failures that, ironically, profit from the appetites and curiosities of the developed world's disposable income while disregarding the crises of hunger and poverty within the developing world. McDonald's is financially well off enough to see such failed innovations—regardless of the individuals and the regions it may offend—as exercises in developing menu items. In the end, failure of this sort is a minor blemish on the reputation of McDonald's taste for tasteless advertisement.

CHAPTER 17

Microsoft Zune

Did you know that there was an early competitor to the beloved Apple iPod? It is indeed true; its name was the Zune, and in the late summer of 2009 it was described like this:

> The Microsoft Zune HD is a beautiful device—inside and out—that presents one of the first appealing and affordable alternatives to the Apple iPod Touch. Microsoft deserves praise for taking the Zune's music and video experience beyond the standard set by Apple. What remains to be seen is whether people will value Microsoft's premium media experience enough to resist the increasingly multipurpose appeal of the iPod.[1]

If the name Zune doesn't ring a bell, you may not be alone. A onetime rival to Apple's digital media technology, Microsoft's Zune was introduced in 2006— and, in one way or another, watched its function, accessibility, and range of novel features fall into disuse by 2011.

Today, the Zune has become the butt of jokes about failed technology, with references turning up in such popular television programs as *The Simpsons, Two and a Half Men, The Big Bang Theory,* and *Silicon Valley.* The Zune even had an almost-political moment when Zack Galifianakis, on his comedy show *Between Two Ferns,* interviewed President Barack Obama. Playing the indifferent political neophyte, Galifianakis is asked by Obama if he's ever heard of his signature Affordable Care Act; Galifianakis replies, "Oh, yeah, I heard about that. That's the thing that doesn't work. Why would you get the guy who created the Zune to make your Web site?"[2]—a witty swipe at the chaotic launch of the online presence of the Affordable Care Act.

Even Hollywood jumped on the bandwagon. In 2017 the much-anticipated Marvel sequel *Guardians of the Galaxy Vol. 2* incorporated a quip about the Zune itself. As Gwynne Watkins explains,

> The obsolete digital music device makes an appearance towards the end of the Marvel blockbuster, after hero Peter Quill (Chris Pratt) has lost his beloved Sony Walkman. Without giving too much away, the Zune is a gift to Quill from a loved one, and Quill is astonished to learn that it holds "300 songs"—a whole lot more than he'd been packing with those Awesome Mix cassette tapes. The joke is that you'd have to literally be living on another planet to get excited about a Zune.[3]

Even more jabs at the Zune ended up in the film's deleted scenes. One, released by *Entertainment Tonight*, featured Kraglin (Sean Gunn) teaching Quill how to operate the Zune, prefacing his instructions by characterizing it as something "made by primitive people."[4] Microsoft was reportedly not amused. According to Comicbook.com's Jay Jason, "[D]uring James Gunn's recent Facebook Q&A, the filmmaker said that he reached out to Microsoft about putting the Zune in the film and the company informed [Gunn] it was unhappy that the Zune was being used in a disparaging manner."[5]

Although Apple technology eventually outstripped Microsoft's popularity, the Zune was actually relatively hip in its early days. ©*iStock/Pinkypills*

In defense of Microsoft, the company's sensitivity about the image of one of its failed products does have merit; the Zune really did have great potential and was once anything but a joke. In the early stages of its development, Microsoft teamed up with Toshiba for manufacturing, basing the Zune's look on Toshiba's Gigabeat S.[6] An early product competing with Apple's iPod, the Zune had a 30-gigabyte hard drive and a three-inch screen, and Microsoft offered Zune Marketplace, similar to Apple's iTunes, where consumers could purchase songs for 99¢ a pop. The first-generation Zune also had some unique features: it came preloaded with songs from record labels like Astralwerks Records, Ninja Tune, DTS, Quango Music Group, Virgin Records, Playlouderecordings, and Sub Pop Records; it also featured wireless song sharing that allowed users to listen for free for up to three days before having to pay for songs.

Still no laughing matter in its early stages, the Zune's next three generations were equally progressive in terms of development. The second generation introduced two smaller models—4- and 8-gigabyte versions—and added a touch-sensitive Zune Pad to replaced the earlier model's somewhat clumsy navigation wheel. The third generation featured 16- and 120-gigabyte versions—the latter, one of the largest capacities on the market for that time. And the fourth generation brought the model up to speed with other displays on the market by offering a high definition (HD) version. By the end of its final product line—the Zune HD—Microsoft's media technology remained Apple's strongest competitor, according to Donald Bell:

> As the high-profile underdog alternative to Apple's iPod portable media player, the Zune has endured an unfair share of jokes and scorn. Proving the adage that "what doesn't kill you, makes you stronger," Microsoft has taken four years'-worth of hard knocks and forged the Zune HD. As one of the only iPod alternatives that can match the iPod Touch in beauty and pricing, the 16GB ($199), 32GB ($269), and 64GB ($349) Zune HD also includes a unique stable of features worthy of Apple's envy.[7]

Within two years after this review, however, Microsoft threw in the towel and effectively conceded victory to Apple. It seems the Cult of Mac had prevailed.

So how did a product with as much potential as the Zune go down in history as the eternal second best? This story of failure is more about Microsoft's unwillingness to remain in that second-place role to Apple, and in the end, Microsoft's decision to pull the plug on the Zune may have been less about its potential and more about wise and prescient insight that being the only real competitor may be profitable only if there's a narrow enough margin between first and second.

Like an aspiring actor or actress struggling to launch a career, from the very start the Zune was hit with criticisms about everything from its weight and appearance to its image in the popular media. Some found the Zune to be a bit too cumbersome: "Users and reviewers are discovering that the Zune is a little too bulky and heavy. As Palm discovered long ago, a large device can feel smaller if the designers round off the edges. Microsoft ignores this lesson of gadget history, with its boxy, blocky design."[8]

Cumbersome it may have been, but it was not egregiously larger than the first-generation iPod. In fact, what were considered to be the Zune's failures in this regard were only slightly different from Apple's more successful features.

Others made a big deal about its actual color. The brown-colored casing didn't sit well with some consumers, and it rubbed at least one blogger the wrong way:

> In person, the device has a rich, warm color. The green tinge is innovative; I've never seen a consumer electronics device that tries for such a complicated, organic palette, and it's pulled off wonderfully. But instead of calling the color chocolate, or something else compelling and attractive, they named it *brown*, a color that has few positive associations except (possibly) UPS. Chocolate is desirable, and fuels passions. It's even a little bit sinful. Hell, you could play on the brown and green theme and call the color "tree."

But no, the color name is prosaic. And worse, it's a color combination that looks terrible on the Web. . . . The failure of brown represents a more profound problem with the Zune: a lack of vision.[9]
To be fair, the Zune was available in white and black, but that it also came in brown was another strike, albeit rather petty, against the new gadget.

Not fully sold on the color thesis, I dug deeper, and in researching why the Zune failed, it became increasingly clear that the problem was less that the Zune failed, as much as it was that its competitor succeeded. In other words, Zune's fall is more accurately explained by Apple's rise to the top of consumers' preferences. Even the mere rhetorical comparison seems to pan the Zune:

> Microsoft has just launched the Zune, which will be one of the most popular digital music players ever made, and *could* have been considered a wild success as a result. Instead, the device has been inevitably and irrevocably compared to Apple's iPod, and thus anything less than becoming a cultural icon will be considered failure.[10]

The very existence of the Apple product made it difficult for any product to envision topping it in popularity, and when comparing any product with Apple, consumers just can't help but bolster the entitlement Apple enjoys—anything second is, in reality, a far second.

Robbie Bach, the former president of Microsoft's Entertainment and Device Division, offered up some insight into the Zune's demise in an interview with *Business Insider* in early 2012. According to Bach, one of the problems was that Zune's advertising schema failed to capture a large enough base to drive its popularity. On the one hand, the Zune team delivered some "artsy ads that appealed to a very small segment of the music space, and we didn't captivate the broad segment of music listeners."[11] But on the other hand, Zune simply couldn't compete with Apple's established business agreements with the music industry. As Bach explains:

> [The music industry] was so hooked on the drug of what Apple was supplying them that they couldn't see past that to realize that they needed something else to actually drive their business. . . . If you look at business value, Apple took whatever business value was in the label business and erased it. That's not a complaint about Apple, good for them.[12]

Yet not everyone considered an expert in this type of technology was convinced the Zune and the iPod were so different. According to Farhad Manjoo, technology columnist for the *New York Times*, the Zune was "just as good as an iPod—it performed all of that device's main functions pretty well. But there's no way in which it [was] *better* than an iPod. And that's why it was doomed." Manjoo explains:

> The first Zune was released in 2006, five years after the iPod's release. The Zune HD came out in 2009, two years after the iPod Touch went on sale. By that point, iPod had become the world's de facto digital entertainment device. To beat it, Microsoft needed to offer something that would make Apple's device look pitifully old-fashioned. The Zune HD didn't do that. Its design marked it as being different from an iPod, but that was pretty much the only difference. There was no reason to buy the Zune unless you wanted to stand apart from the Apple cult. And there was a cost to standing apart from Apple: Because of its popularity, there were millions of apps and accessories for the iPod. As good as it was, the Zune HD couldn't match Apple's sheer market power.[13]

For Manjoo, the perfect storm of popularity, infrastructure, innovation, and the sheer advantage of being the first in the field made Apple invincible, leaving the Zune without a chance in the world of conquering the iPod in terms of market share.

Everyday critics chimed in as well. On the question-and-answer website Quora, the prompt: "Why did the iPod succeed while the Zune failed?" garnered some interesting responses. One critic believed the failure could be chalked up to the Zune's inability to "reinvent the wheel" to its advantage; that is, if Apple had already created something really incredible, why would anyone want to renavigate the learning curve for something apparently inferior to what Apple had already established:

> To be competitive, Zune needed to be cheaper and better. Zune was marginally cheaper, but nowhere better. Along with strong product appeal, the iPod had a first-mover advantage. If you bought an iPod, you weren't going to buy a Zune. If you were upgrading, you would rather upgrade to a newer iPod since all your songs were trapped in iTunes. This sort of user-lock-in is great for business but lousy for consumers. Consumer inertia also played a role—the iPod worked really well so there was little reason to take a gamble on yet another unproven gadget.[14]

In some ways, in this binary view, having an iPod simply meant not having a Zune, and Apple's early arrival on the scene meant that those most invested in this technology were going to remain invested in their original investment.

Instead of focusing on where the Zune had failed, another critic focused squarely on what Apple had accomplished. The absence of any follow-up highlighting redeeming qualities of the Zune spoke volumes by literally not speaking at all. Rattling off Apple's features in bullet points, this critic stated:

- It was (and still is) well designed and it excelled with ease of use through its vastly superior user interface to contemporary MP3 players.
- When the original device was released in 2001, it fit 1000 songs into your pocket, while still being small and light.
- It offered simple music discovery, purchase, and syncing to a device through iTunes. More importantly, it worked with Windows computers as well.
- Apple allowed third party companies to make accessories for iPods, hence they enabled it to widespread into fitness, automobile, speaker, case and other markets.[15]

Sometimes, as in this case, the absence of criticism is as powerful as criticism itself. The upshot: Apple was simply superior, and the argument about whether anything—or nothing at all—even came close was futile.

Finally, one individual simply saw the Zune as coming up short at a point in the development of media technology when Apple had already monopolized the field:

In short, [the Zune was] too little, too late, and too much an obvious effort to do the same thing Apple was already doing, without providing any really strong incentives to go the Microsoft way instead. To me, it seemed like a product that really only appealed to people who hate Apple and/or love Microsoft.[16]

Interestingly enough, what of these responses capture, in sum, is the sentiment that the iPod is an actual experience, while the Zune was simply a product.

Some analysts were far more biting in their critiques. In a 2011 Chautauqua Institution lecture delivered by Dev Patnaik, CEO of Jump Associates, the Zune is the focus of a case study on failure. Patnaik describes the Zune as "slow," "clunky," and "hard to use," adding that one reviewer commented, "[T]he process of installing the Microsoft Zune on your computer is about as pleasurable as having an airbag explode in your face."[17] Speaking in terms of consumer purchase, Patnaik notes that the Zune sold a mere 2 million units worldwide in its first eighteen months, in contrast to Apple's sales of more than 84 million units in that same period.

Yet aside from the opinions about less-than-desirable hardware, cumbersome installation, and differences in profit margins, Patnaik attributes the Zune's failure to a lack of understanding about what consumers really wanted. Before introducing the Zune as a case study in failure, Patnaik prefaces his segment by describing one of Microsoft's huge successes: the Xbox. According to Patnaik, the Xbox championed consumer interest by relating to the people themselves, tapping into the "man-boy" sentiment of gamers. This, however, was in 2001, five years before the launch of the Zune, at which point designers failed to exhibit that same sense of empathy. There just wasn't a battle cry waiting to lead the charge for the Zune's success.

Ultimately, Microsoft's decision to cut its losses and put the brakes on the Zune was, by all accounts, a smart business move. Being second to a product like the overwhelmingly popular technology of Apple is only worthwhile if it's a narrow second. That Microsoft realized that sooner rather than later—within a period of roughly five years—is truly a victory. With the increasing prominence of Apple and its never-ending stream newer, better, faster, sleeker, and more advanced products surfacing annually, the failure of the Zune in the short run will be nothing less than a hindsight success in the long run.

CHAPTER 18

Google Wave

Despite the overwhelming success of Microsoft, the computing and software development corporation has certainly had its share of products that went bust. From the pesky little animated icons of desktop assistants such as Microsoft Bob and Clippit to the portable multimedia player Zune that (as discussed in chapter 17) simply could not compete with Apple's iPod, Microsoft's shortcomings demonstrate that even a tech industry giant is not exempt from failure.

Nowhere are these failures more apparent than through some of Microsoft's operating systems. Windows Vista—perhaps only second on the list of the worst computer operating systems next to Millennium Edition—was introduced 2006 and was touted as the next generation of the extremely successful Windows XP. However, criticism immediately poured in. Everything from claims of slow processing and vulnerable security issues to complaints that it was overpriced confronted Microsoft's new system. Windows 7 was released in 2009, less than three years later, making Windows Vista another obsolete operating system.

But this chapter is not about Microsoft's failures or even the case of Windows Vista, but rather about the highly innovative internet company Google and its failed all-in-one, Google Wave. Research about Google Wave, however, is not easy to come by. This, for example, is what you'll find if you search the company's website:

> As we announced in August 2010, we are not continuing active development of Google Wave as a stand-alone product. Google Wave will be shut down in April 2012. This page details the implication of the turn down process for Google Wave.[1]

Although there are plenty of examples of technology failures—mostly due to obsolescence—few dive into disuse as quickly and inconspicuously as Google

Wave did. To be sure, it's rare that big-name companies like Google, with enormous development budgets and personnel, experience such blemishes on their record of successful achievements. Yet if we were to separate the technological innovators—in this case, Google—from the failed technology—Google Wave—it becomes apparent that we as consumers have a greater impact on the success or failure of technology than we might presume. As digital communication is operationalized by our practice, not solely a product or production that develops independent of our interaction, the way in which we utilize a particular technology may serve as at least one predictor of how well it will fare in the long run.

To be honest, I never actually used a Google Wave account, and as these accounts are virtually gone,[2] there is no way for me to experience its functionality. Unlike other failures highlighted in this book, which left behind a substantial record of their existence, the Wave—its successes, its failures, and most of the positive and negative criticism it generated—has just about vanished. For these reasons, re-creating the life and death of Google Wave is critical to understanding that which in this case simply is no longer around to understand.

To begin, what was Google Wave? The short answer is that it was an e-mail software framework designed to bring e-mail up to speed with more current technology associated with the internet. The long answer is more complicated, perhaps even bit mind-boggling, but nonetheless actually quite interesting: Google Wave was a highly versatile e-mail software designed to host a single message to which multiple parties could contribute in real time. According to Lars Rasmussen, one of its developers, Google Wave was an attempt to use e-mail as if it were created in a more contemporary context. At the Wave's debut event, Rasmussen offered up this explanation: "When we started this project more than two years ago, we asked ourselves the question: What would e-mail look like if it was invented today? And obviously there are about a million ways you can try to answer that question. What you're going to see today, Google Wave, is our attempt."[3] With an audience full of developers, Rasmussen went on to offer each of them an account—the first of three circulations of the Wave.

With the introduction complete and developers testing it out, Google Wave was literally on its way: new, exciting, and unique. What made Google Wave such a hit was that it provided a single e-mail conversation in a hosted format that allowed multiple participants to contribute. So, for example, if I wanted to discuss this book with my editors as well as my colleagues, I might post a message titled "Failure in Popular Culture," and then invite all parties to contribute. These parties would then have the opportunity to chime in on the discussion, and their input would be displayed in real time. A number of additional bells and whistles would add to the experience, including an option to drag and drop an assortment of attachments into the discussion, link the discussion to any number of blogs or other social media pages, and a playback option that allowed participants to explore the development of the discussion at any time. With its commitment to make electronic communication more of a communal experience, Google Wave also featured the Rosy Etta robot translation software, allowing for seamless communication between individuals typing in different languages.

Boasting such novel features, Google Wave appeared to be a real innovation in communication technology, yet in just under three years Google had suspended its development. When it was initially released in May 2009, access was limited only to developers. Google then followed up in September of that same year with a limited release to 100,000 users, with an option for those individuals to invite others. But it would be another eight months before Google finally released it to the general public; in August 2010, Google abruptly began closing the curtains on its development, and by spring of 2012 Google Wave was shut down altogether.

So what went wrong with Wave? There wasn't a whole lot of explanation from Google, and it would seem that, as T. S. Eliot might have remarked, Google Wave's end arrived not with a bang but a whimper. In what appears

Rarely ever making mention of its shortcomings, Google's image of success has gone well beyond technological innovation, even spilling into the world of Hollywood's popular culture. The 2013 film *The Internship* featured Vince Vaughn (left) and Owen Wilson (right) attempting to cut their losses as failed salesmen and compete with younger, tech-savvy interns at Google. *Twentieth Century Fox Film Corporation/Photofest © Twentieth Century Fox Film Corporation*

to be amateur footage of Google CEO Eric Schmidt sitting down with several reporters, Schmidt explains what he thinks put the brakes on Google Wave: "What happened was we liked the UI and we liked a lot of the new features in it, but it didn't get enough traction, so we're taking that technology and applying it to new technologies."[4] This sounds fair enough, and, true to Schmidt's words, not only did some of the features find a home in other Google products, but the development of the Wave didn't actually die as much it was placed in the hands of the Apache Software Foundation for further development. It did, however, fail in its initial run, and that—with a product that had such enormous public visibility and thus the potential to be such a major success—constitutes a kind of subjective failure of epic proportions.

Although it would be a daunting task to pinpoint the exact reason for the failure of this type of technology, one popular social theory associated with class and social preferences might shed some light on how Google Wave became obsolete. In 1979, French sociologist Pierre Bourdieu published *Distinction: A Social Critique of the Judgment of Taste*, a seminal piece on the dynamics of how social dispositions are informed by one's socialization through class. In what is considered one of the most intellectual interpretations of social interaction, Bourdieu introduces his ongoing research on *fields*, those settings in which social interaction takes place in accordance with certain organizational, rule-oriented, or regulatory structures. These fields can be institutional—like religion, education, politics, and the like—or they can be leisurely environments such as parks, bars, or restaurants. Basically, a field can be any setting that may be defined as such, but what's more important than defining a field is interpreting what type of symbolic possessions individuals bring to a given field in order to navigate through it. Each of us possess a battery knowledge and skills we have acquired through our socialization, all of which serves to form what Bourdieu calls one's *habitus*, or the disposition that comprises our individuality and allows us to interact as such within a field. Bourdieu argues that habitus is thus made up of an inventory of capital, including economic capital or financial disposables; social capital, which refers to how one knows how to interact with others; and cultural capital, a kind of portfolio of material and nonmaterial culture that one has acquired and appears to be well versed in through extensive socialization. These forms of capital are then transformed into symbolic capital within a field setting, allowing individuals to utilize all their capital possessions to their advantage.

So how does this relate to Google Wave? To begin, think of the internet as a field. In this field people bring their various forms of capital to the junctions of technology and digital communication. In today's world of digital communication, there are infinite examples of how one's habitus mediates experience. When we visit social media sites, contribute to a blog, log on to our e-mail accounts, and the like, we're actually entering into relatively discernible fields in which we employ our individual inventories of capital. The economic capital that allows us to access to various sites, complete downloads, and shop online is a testament to how money can enhance—or, in its absence, hinder—our experience within an internet field. Additionally, the exposure to various intellectual and technological conditioning that serves as knowledge about how to use the internet is a demonstration of our cultural capital at play. Moreover, our social capital is quite readily obvious through the way we network with others on the internet, especially with communication channels such as Facebook, Twitter, Pinterest, and, of course, good old-fashioned e-mail. As all these forms of capital transform into symbolic capital through expression and interaction, they can only be accounted for in symbolic terms. So, to provide a rather generic example, think about how an upbringing in an environment of wealth, with exposure to vast amounts of reading material and computers, as well as the company of others who had similar upbringings, might affect one's experience of engaging in digital communication compared with the experience of an individual who was raised in a rural environment with very little wealth, no similar amenities, and in relative isolation from others. Of course, if this comparison is based upon assumptions, it might generate equally generic differences in perceived experience, yet it is only in actual practice, while engaged in the field, that the symbolic nuances of these disparities become apparent.

As the variety and abstract characteristics of these forms of capital through habitus aren't really measurable, much less calculable in their distinct forms, it is only in practice that one may really view how they operate. For this reason, Bourdieu finds this notion of practice within the field to be central to the dynamics of human interaction. As he explains,

> Because it can only account for practices by bringing to light successively the series of effects which underlie them, analysis initially conceals the structure of the life-style characteristic of an agent or class of agents, that is, the unity hidden under the diversity and multiplicity of the set of practices performed in fields governed by different logics and therefore inducing different forms of realization, in accordance with the formula [(habitus) (capital)] + field = practice. It also conceals the structure of the symbolic space marked out by the whole set of these structured practices, all the distinct and distinctive life-styles which are always defined objectively and sometimes subjectively in and through their mutual relationships.[5]

For Bourdieu, the only way to view a more complete picture of this interaction is to highlight how practice materializes. Literally, he argues, "one must return to the practice-unifying and practice-generating principle, i.e., class habitus, the internalized form of class condition and of the conditioning it entails."[6]

The way in which practice materialized among individuals participating in the initial circulation round of Google Wave forecast the eventual end of its development: people were simply unclear as to how they should be using the new technology. For example, Gina Trapani, coauthor of *The Complete Guide to Google Wave*, may be one of very few to offer up a logical explanation of Google Wave's failure. In early August 2009, Trapani posted a summative account of the questions she fielded just after Wave's collapse. To one general question about why Google's new product failed, Trapani responded, "Wave simply didn't attract the user base it should have. The tool didn't explain itself well enough. The barriers to entry were just too high. The use cases weren't clear. People didn't get it. One million active users wasn't enough in the Google universe."[7]

At the heart of Trapani's response the exclusivity Google Wave presented. In many ways, the accessibility issues Trapani focuses on are rather telling and certainly germane to Bourdieu's notion of social capital. Users weren't in the know about how to proceed with its use because they weren't engaged in the practice of using it—a socialization process that lends itself to building social capital. The rub is that users would have to have had some amount of practice or interaction with others in order to have familiarized themselves with the ins and outs of the new technology, yet in the early days, which could certainly be considered its formative stages, Google Wave was simply not accessible to all.

Take, for example, the limited availability of Google Wave during this formative stage, when it was offered exclusively to developers. The initial Google Wave accounts were available only to developers, but was this the population that had the most influence on its success? After all, developers develop, and although they might prioritize the development of this flashy new technology, wouldn't they be more attuned to communicating on the reliable accounts they were already using? I assume developers engage in a rather high volume of communication for their vocation, and the use of a new and perhaps unpredictable technology might not be the best investment of their time. Communication is incredibly important, and in order to preserve the flow of such communication, it is crucial that one stay affiliated with that which has all of one's contacts and intact.

It seems that the initial inaccessibility of Wave may have been one of Google's missteps. One post on Mashable.com includes reports—accompanied by an actual screenshot, no less—demonstrating how those seeking to take part in Wave had innovated with their networking resources. As the story explains, one initial invitee actually listed his or her invitation status in an auction on eBay:

> Haven't received your Google Wave Invite yet? You're not alone. Thousands of users around the world are still awaiting their invitation to Google's new communication platform. At this point, it's not clear whether demand far exceeds supply or Google is simply still

waiting to open the flood gates, but if you really can't wait, at least one invite has already found its way to eBay. The item has already attracted 19 bids, pushing the price up to $70.[8]

Although it's difficult to discern the ratio of humor to seriousness in this example, it does suggest that there was a demand that wasn't being met.

Like all fields of interaction, what people bring to the field is just as important as what the field offers to them. But without the skill set and knowledge of how to navigate a given field, the field could prove useless to its participants. Even if one has accumulated enough cultural and economic capital to fare well in similar fields, within the emergence of a new technology no amount of cultural or economic capital compares to the value of the social capital necessary for acquiring knowledge of how things will work. Social capital is imperative to knowing how to utilize a communication tool that depends upon one's familiarity with how it functions among and between others. It was there, amid the field of digital communication running through the internet, where those deprived of such a repertoire of social capital could do little more than symbolically wave good-bye to Google Wave.

Conclusion

This book is primarily intended to be a sociological text, yet unlike the methodological principles of striving to maintain a modicum of objectivity, I exercised various subjective liberties in an attempt to be true to what I believe is fascinating about the phenomenon of failure. In addition to designating certain products and productions from popular culture as failures, I have also taken the further step of criticizing and at times ridiculing these failures. However, I indulge in this disparagement not because I believe casting judgment upon such instances is conducive to an intellectual discussion about failure, but rather because it demonstrates the type of sentiment often felt by the audiences that have observed it and the individuals who have experienced it. To exclude such commentary in light of what I have seen to be a consistent pattern of contempt for a lack of honorable achievement, would be to treat, defend, or even advocate for failure in the same way success is so commonly safeguarded, encouraged, and prized.

As a member of the society I write about, I cannot easily separate myself from those complex nuances that make up the experience of failing in the face of striving for success. In fact, if failure is so simplistically determined by a lack of success, I consider myself a genuine failure. Looking back on my own life, I can certainly say that I have experienced much more failure than success, yet not only am I quite comfortable with this record of shortcomings, I am also well aware of the fact that the failure I have experienced, including the type of failure discussed in this book, is socially constructed—it is simply not natural. Failure is only such due to the way success is defined, and neither failure nor success exist independently; instead they depend entirely upon each other's existence. It follows, then, that the only natural thing about failure and success is that they are related within a nexus of communication that humans use to describe what they would like to see and experience in contrast to what they would not.

In this way, if one wants a more realistic understanding of failure, it is important to find a way to view the stigma that is so often attached to it as equally artificial as the abovementioned label *natural*. In looking beyond this stigma and disregarding any notion of naturalness, one may be better able to understand the true quality of failure.

For myself, this understanding affects not only the way I view failure, but also how I engage in a discourse about it. My participation in this discourse is thus informed through a realistic vein, certainly not that which one might find in some inspirational infomercial. In other words, I cannot imagine myself writing about failure through some tone of moral entrepreneurship, delivering a pep talk to the unsuccessful and reminding audiences that the bar of accomplishment should be set high, or even modestly encouraging people to seek success through their products or productions. This would be uncharacteristic of my own beliefs; it would be what I have always viewed as the wrong direction for delivering any type of message. Telling someone to "get back up and brush yourself off" after a fall of any degree may sound nice, thoughtful, and even appropriate, yet I have to wonder at what cost such a message comes. Moreover, do messages like these really suggest something about the failure of the failed, or is it more attuned to the failure of the audience to experience comfort and acceptance in viewing failure? Such messages certainly imply something about values associated with capitalist modes of production—and more importantly, competition, the cornerstone of all work ethic bound to it. In reality, however, heartwarming statements about failure that encourage individuals to keep going and try harder serve largely to reinforce socially constructed standards of what constitutes success. To succeed at an endeavor requires that there be some built-in opportunity to execute something up to the standards of those who have defined success or to regard such standards as so universal that they continually replicate them— not to mention the varying degrees to which success implies the exceeding of expectations in order to be singled out as one of the very best at a given endeavor.

Conversely, my opinion of any set standards about achieving success is fairly poor, and I would not give much thought, much less any time, to encouraging people to follow them simply because they exist. Instead, taking a minute to view how one attempts success, understanding the possible outcomes, and then realizing that failure is indeed one of these outcomes, is in my mind much more appropriate than blindly encouraging individuals to go forward, do whatever it takes to win, be number one, and the like. Rather than beginning with the audacious premise that success is the only option—or at least the only admirable one—it might be more suitable for the social psychology of a community to focus upon *effort* as a means to an end, as opposed to focusing on success as an end in and of itself. If this were more popularly practiced, failure might shed some of its negative stigma and be viewed as something that simply happens.

To this end, encouraging the acceptance of failure, in contrast to discouraging it as unacceptable, retools the potential for a more positive symbolic interaction in the face of failure.

In this book I wanted to explore not only the notion of failure as it relates to popular culture, but also the quirky narratives that have sprung up all around it. Although there will always be official narratives of the demise of a given product or production, there are also unofficial accounts that contribute to the humorous and lively legacy of those things that missed their intended marks. Throughout this book I asked, What *might* have caused a failure? I speculated about the ironies of how a particular failure may have led to the success of something else. I explored how failure looks, how it feels, and to what extent it really is what we think it is. Yet regardless of my inquiry, in order to open up a further discussion about how failure materializes, I tried to apply a theoretical framework to each case mentioned herein—or at the very least advance some reasonable speculation that conjures up a much more critical form of thinking about such phenomena. Of course, such application is not meant to be in any way definitive, but rather a method of framing a discussion in sociocultural terms for audiences to ponder, build upon, or even reject entirely; in any such case, the objective of generating a discussion should be met. To the extent that I have attempted as much, my hope is that failure within popular culture was appreciated within the pages you have just turned.

Notes

Introduction

1. Jon Ronson, "Psycho Dabble," *This American Life*, July 10, 2009, podcast audio, https://www.thisamericanlife.org/385/pro-se/act-one-0.
2. American Psychiatric Association, "307.47 Nightmare Disorder (formerly Dream Anxiety Disorder)," in *Diagnostic and Statistical Manual of Mental Disorders*, 4th ed., text revision (Arlington, VA: American Psychiatric Publishing, 2000), 631–34.
3. Phil Dusenbury, *Then We Set His Hair on Fire: Insights and Accidents from a Hall-of-Fame Career in Advertising* (New York: Penguin, 2005), 234.
4. Douglas C. McGill, "'Smokeless' Cigarette's Hapless Start," *New York Times*, November 19, 1988.
5. Matt Haig, *Brand Failures: The Truth about the 100 Biggest Branding Mistakes of All Time* (London: Kogen Page, 2003), 51.
6. Scott A. Sandage, *Born Losers: A History of Failure in America* (Cambridge, MA: Harvard University Press, 2005), 1.
7. Sandage, *Born Losers*, 1.

Chapter 1

1. Thomas A. Bonsall, *Disaster in Dearborn: The Story of the Edsel* (Palo Alto, CA: Stanford University Press, 2002), 1.
2. Perhaps most notable among this bunch was Robert S. McNamara. Long before presenting the case to Congress for the escalation of combat in Vietnam as secretary of defense under President Lyndon B. Johnson, McNamara helped to organize the management of the Ford Motor Company. For a detailed account of McNamara's involvement, as well as that of the Whiz Kids, see John A. Bryne, *Whiz Kids: The Founding Fathers of American Business and the Legacy They Left Us* (New York: Doubleday, 1993).

3. Martin J. Smith and Patrick J. Kiger, *Poplorica: A Popular History of the Fads, Mavericks, Inventions and Lore That Shaped Modern America* (New York: Harper Resource, 2004), 134.

4. Smith and Kiger, *Poplorica*, 130.

5. Bonsall, *Disaster in Dearborn*, 126.

6. Tom Dicke, "The Edsel: Forty Years as a Symbol of Failure," *Journal of Popular Culture* 43, no. 3 (2010): 486.

7. Dicke, "The Edsel," 486.

8. Dicke, "The Edsel," 493–94.

9. Howard S. Becker, *Outsiders: Studies in the Sociology of Deviance* (New York: Macmillan, 1963), 9.

10. Pam Scholder Ellen and Paula Fitzgerald Bone, "Stained by the Label: Stigma and the Case of Genetically Modified Foods," *Journal of Public Policy & Marketing* 27, no. 1 (2008): 70.

11. Ellen and Bone, "Stained by the Label," 72.

Chapter 2

1. Dan Epstein, *Big Hair and Plastic Grass: A Funky Ride through Baseball and America in the Swinging '70s* (New York: Thomas Dunne Books, 2010), 243.

2. Thorstein Veblen, *The Theory of the Leisure Class: An Economic Study of Institutions* (New York: Mentor Books, 1953), 41–46.

3. Epstein, *Big Hair and Plastic Grass*, 13.

4. Epstein, *Big Hair and Plastic Grass*, 2.

5. Epstein, *Big Hair and Plastic Grass*, 111.

6. Chuck Sudo, "The Chicagoist Flashback: The White Sox Don Shorts for the First Time," *Chicagoist*, August 8, 2012, http://chicagoist.com/2012/08/08/the_chicago ist_flashback_the_white.php.

7. Epstein, *Big Hair and Plastic Grass*, 111.

8. "1996 Means Kentucky, Converse and Those Denim Unis," *Lost Lettermen*, 1996, http://www.lostlettermen.com/lost-uniforms-1996-means-kentucky-converse -and-those-denim-unis (December 5, 2014).

9. George Ritzer, *Classical Sociological Theory* (New York: McGraw-Hill, 2000), 333.

10. In a closely related concept, Veblen introduces what he calls *conspicuous consumption*, needless consumption for the sake of establishing one's image as wealthy and thus able to make purchases without regard for a budget. See Veblen, *The Theory of the Leisure Class*, 60–80.

11. Veblen, *The Theory of the Leisure Class*, 22.

12. Erin Sorensen, "Longhorns Practice Uniforms Are Almost as Bad as Auburn's," *Bleacher Report*, August 6, 2012, http://bleacherreport.com/articles/1287054-texas -football-longhorns-practice-uniforms-are-almost-as-bad-as-auburns (December 20, 2014).

Chapter 3

1. Luis Cabral and David Backus, "Betamax and VHS," Firms and Markets Mini Case, New York University, Leonard N. Stern School of Business, 2002, 1, http://pages .stern.nyu.edu/~lcabral/teaching/betamax.pdf.

2. Michael Cusumano, Yiorgos Mylonadis, and Richard Rosenbloom, "Strategic Maneuvering and Mass-Market Dynamic: The Triumph of VHS over Beta," *Business History Review* 66 (1992): 60.

3. Cusumano, Mylonadis, and Rosenbloom, "Strategic Maneuvering and Mass-Market Dynamic," 57.

4. Ian Rowley, "Next-Gen DVD's Porn Struggle," *Bloomberg Businessweek*, January 22, 2007, http://www.businessweek.com/stories/2007-01-22/next-gen-dvds-porn-strug glebusinessweek-business-news-stock-market-and-financial-advice.

5. From the Sony Super Betamax Digital Promotion Tape. This promotion tape, cut in 1987, was used to market Beta models SL-HF860D, SL-HF840D, and SL-810D. It was produced by the Sony Video Communications Center in Park Ridge, New Jersey.

6. Sony Super Betamax Digital Promotion Tape.

Chapter 4

1. Matthew Honan, "The Best: Obsolete Technologies from the Sundial to the Laser Disc," *Wired*, October 23, 2007, https://www.wired.com/2007/10/st-best-20.

2. Jason Curtis, "LaserDisc (1983–2001)," Museum of Obsolete Media, March 14, 2009, http://www.obsoletemedia.org/laserdisc.

3. Dave Kehr, "Goodbye, DVD. Hello Future," *New York Times*, March 4, 2011, http://www.nytimes.com/2011/03/06/movies/homevideo/06dvds.html.

4. bdevore30, "The Laserdisc Failure: The First Optical Disc Format," Storyfy.com, 2016, https://storify.com/bdevore30/the-laserdisc-failure-57ba652f10948ce140a48dd8.

5. Dennis Hunt, "To Rent or Buy Laser Discs? That Is the Question," *Los Angeles Times*, August 16, 1991, http://articles.latimes.com/1991-08-16/entertainment/ca-590 _1_laser-discs.

Chapter 5

1. Jodi Schorb and Tania Hammidi have researched the mullet rather closely and have acknowledged the difficulties this subjectivity poses. As they have stated, they do not wish for their readers to assume that they "intend to speak as arbiters of style, as defenders of lesbian chic against the threat of the 'unstylish' lesbian that the sho-lo apparently embodies," adding instead that they "question what is at stake when we unquestioningly define beauty." For further discussion, see Jodi Schorb and Tania Hammidi. "Sho-Lo

Showdown: The Do's and Don'ts of Lesbian Chic," *Tulsa Studies in Women's Literature* 19, no. 2 (2000): 257.

2. Charles Kurzman, Chelise Anderson, Clinton Key, Youn Ok Lee, Mairead Moloney, Alexis Silver, and Maria W. Van Ryn, "Celebrity Status," *Sociological Theory* 25, no. 4 (2007): 357.

3. Schorb and Hammidi, "Sho-Lo Showdown," 261.

4. Tania Hammidi and Susan B. Kaiser, "Doing Beauty: Negotiating Lesbian Looks in Everyday Life," in *Lesbians, Levis and Lipstick: The Meaning of Beauty in Our Lives*, ed. Jeanine C. Cogan and Joanie M. Erikson (New York: Harrington Park Press, 1999), 59.

5. Patricia Adler and Peter Adler, "Dynamics of Inclusion and Exclusion in Preadolescent Cliques," *Social Psychology Quarterly* 58, no. 3 (1995): 145–62.

6. David A. Locher, "The Industrial Identity Crisis: The Failure of a Newly Forming Subculture to Identify Itself," in *Youth Culture: Identity in a Postmodern World*, ed. Jonathon S. Epstein (Malden, MA: Blackwell, 1998), 101.

7. Schorb and Hammidi, "Sho-Lo Showdown," 257.

8. See Beastie Boys, "Mullet Head," *Ill Communication* (Grand Royal Records, 1994), compact disc.

9. See the Vandals, "I've Got an Ape Drape," *Hitler Bad, Vandals Good* (Nitro Records, 1998), compact disc.

10. Billy Ray Cyrus, "I Want My Mullet Back," *Wanna Be Your Joe* (New Door Records UM, 2006), compact disc.

11. "Welcome to Rate My Mullet .com!" RateMyMullet.com, http://www.ratemy mullet.com/?page=home.

12. Mary Douglas, *Purity and Danger: An Analysis of Concepts of Pollution and Taboo* (New York: Routledge, 1966), 94.

Chapter 6

1. For an in-depth analysis of this concept, generally known as *commodity self*, see Stuart Ewen, *Captains of Consciousness: Advertising and the Social Roots of Consumer Culture* (New York: Basic Books, 2001), 61–68.

2. "History," BluBlocker, http://www.blublocker.com/pages/history.

3. "Blue Light Has a Dark Side," *Harvard Health Letter*, May 2012, http://www .health.harvard.edu/newsletters/Harvard_Health_Letter/2012/May/blue-light-has-a -dark-side#.

4. Mike Conklin, "Start the Presses, the First Cubs Book Has Been Announced . . .," *Chicago Tribune*, October 17, 1989, http://articles.chicagotribune.com/1989-10-17/ sports/8901230412_1_cubs-big-easy-lineup.

5. Sophie Ewens, "Where to Buy Richie Tenenbaum Sunglasses," *IT News Online*, 2012, http://itonlinenews.com/where-to-buy-richie-tenenbaum-sunglasses.

6. Megan McLachlan, "10 Awesome Sunglasses Inspired by Movies," *Primer*, 2011, http://www.primermagazine.com/2011/spend/10-awesome-sunglasses-inspired-by-movies.

7. "BluBlocker® Sunglasses Get a Special Invite to the Latin Grammy Awards," *Yahoo! Finance*, November 15, 2012, http://finance.yahoo.com/news/blublocker-sunglasses -very-special-invite-213800501.html.

8. Chris Gentilviso, "Blublocker Sunglasses," *Time*, August 18, 2010, http://www .time.com/time/specials/packages/article/0,28804,2011470_2011194_2011181,00.html.

Chapter 7

1. Georg Simmel, "Fashion," *American Journal of Sociology* 62, no. 6 (May 1956): 541.

2. Simmel, "Fashion," 542.

3. Simmel, "Fashion," 541.

4. Simmel, "Fashion," 542–43.

5. Simmel, "Fashion," 549.

6. Herbert Marcuse, "Liberation from the Affluent Society," in *The Dialectics of Liberation*, ed. David Cooper (Baltimore: Penguin, 1968), 180.

7. Victor Lebow, "Price Competition in 1955," *Journal of Retailing* (spring 1955), http://www.gcafh.org/edlab/Lebow.pdf.

8. *The Story of Stuff*, written by Annie Leonard, Louis Fox, and Jonah Sachs; directed by Louis Fox (Washington, DC: Free Range Studios, 2007), http://storyofstuff.org/mov ies/story-of-stuff.

9. Simmel, "Fashion," 548.

10. Elizabeth Licata, "Meet 12 Celebs Who Pull off Harem Pants So Well That You'll Actually Buy a Pair," *Gloss*, May 12, 2014, http://www.thegloss.com/2014/05/16/fash ion/celebrities-harem-pants-how-to-wear-them.

11. Licata, "Meet 12 Celebs."

12. Zubaz, "About," http://www.zubaz.com/pages/about_us.

Chapter 8

1. Mark Pendergrast, *For God, Country and Coca-Cola: The Definitive History of the Great American Soft Drink and the Company That Makes It* (New York: Basic Books, 2004), 352.

2. Rachid Haoues, "30 Years Ago Today, Coca-Cola Made Its Worst Mistake," CBS News, April 23, 2015, https://www.cbsnews.com/news/30-years-ago-today-coca-cola -new-coke-failure.

3. Robert M. Schindler, "The Real Lesson of New Coke: The Value of Focus Groups for Predicting the Effects of Social Influence," *Marketing Research* (December 1992): 23.

4. John S. Demott, "All Afizz over the New Coke," *Time*, June 24, 1985, http:// content.time.com/time/magazine/article/0,9171,959449,00.html.

5. "The Real Story of New Coke," *Coca-Cola Journey*, November 14, 2012, http:// www.coca-colacompany.com/stories/coke-lore-new-coke.

6. James C. Cobb, "What We Can Learn from Coca-Cola's Biggest Blunder," *Time*, July 10, 2015, http://time.com/3950205/new-coke-history-america.

7. "Here's to Gay Mullins, Who Gave His All for The Real Thing—but Hey, Gay, Why Stop with Coke?" *People*, July 29, 1985, http://people.com/archive/heres -to-gay-mullins-who-gave-his-all-for-the-real-thing-but-hey-gay-why-stop-with-coke -vol-24-no-5.

8. Haoues, "30 Years Ago Today, Coca-Cola Made Its Worst Mistake."

9. Ryan Gorman and Skye Gould, "This Mistake from 30 Years Ago Almost Destroyed Coca-Cola," *Business Insider*, April 23, 2015, http://www.businessinsider.com/ new-coke-the-30th-anniversary-of-coca-colas-biggest-mistake-2015-4.

10. Haoues, "30 Years Ago Today, Coca-Cola Made Its Worst Mistake."

11. Gorman and Gould, "This Mistake from 30 Years Ago Almost Destroyed Coca-Cola."

12. Haoues, "30 Years Ago Today, Coca-Cola Made Its Worst Mistake."

13. Gorman and Gould, "This Mistake from 30 Years Ago Almost Destroyed Coca-Cola."

14. Schindler, "The Real Lesson of New Coke," 23.

15. Cobb, "What We Can Learn from Coca-Cola's Biggest Blunder."

16. Stephanie Strom, "Donald R. Keough, Who Led Coca-Cola Through New Coke Debacle, Dies at 88," *New York Times*, February 25, 2015, https://www.nytimes .com/2015/02/25/business/donald-r-keough-who-led-coca-cola-through-new-coke -debacle-dies-at-88.html.

Chapter 9

1. Bob Garfield, "Why Make Bud Dry an Antidote to Life's Problems? Don't Ask," *Advertising Age* (October 1, 1990): 58.

2. The role of the phrase rhyming even permeated popular culture, winding up as a little-known lyrical line in the rap song "All My Love" by House of Pain in 1992: "Can ya keep a secret, so can I. Why ask why, try bud dry, I get fly smokin' a thai." The line's inclusion in the song did appear to establish the rhyme effect, but lyrically was as insignificant in this song as it was in the commercial message from Bud Dry.

3. Garfield, "Why Make Bud Dry an Antidote to Life's Problems?" 58.

4. Ira Teinowitz, "Bud Dry Pitches Women," *Advertising Age* (July 1, 1991): 10.

5. Garfield, "Why Make Bud Dry an Antidote to Life's Problems?" 58.

Chapter 10

1. "Pepsi Will Market-Test a Clear-Colored Cola: Retailing: It Could Expand the $46-Billion Soft Drink Market, Analysts Say," *Los Angeles Times*, April 13, 1992, http:// articles.latimes.com/1992-04-13/business/fi-244_1_soft-drink.

2. Matt Haig, *Brand Failures: The Truth about the 100 Biggest Branding Mistakes of All Time* (London: Kogan Page, 2003), 43.

3. Lawrence L. Garber Jr. and Eve M. Hyatt, "Color as a Tool for Visual Persuasion," in *Persuasive Imagery: A Consumer Response Perspective*, ed. Linda M. Scott and Rajeev Batra (Mahwah, NJ: Routledge, 2003), 313.

4. Brendan Koerner, "The Long, Slow, Torturous Death of Zima: Fourteen Years after its Death, Zima Is Finally at Peace," *Slate*, November 26, 2008, http://www.slate.com/articles/life/drink/2008/11/the_long_slow_torturous_death_of_zima.html.

5. "Coors Enters Bottled Water Market," *New York Times*, January 16, 1990, http://www.nytimes.com/1990/01/16/business/coors-enters-bottled-water-market.html.

6. Kate Bonamici Flaim, "The Education of an Accidental CEO: Lessons Learned from the Trailer Park to the Corner Office," *Fast Company*, October 1, 2007, http://www.fastcompany.com/60555/winging-it.

7. Adam Bryant, "Coke Adds a New Cola to Its 'New Age' Stable," *New York Times*, December 15, 1992, http://www.nytimes.com/1992/12/15/business/company-news-coke-adds-a-clear-cola-to-its-new-age-stable.html.

8. Melinda C. Blackman and Collen A. Kvoska, *Nutrition Psychology: Improving Dietary Adherence* (Sudbury, MA: Jones and Bartlett, 1992), 92.

9. Lawrence L. Garber Jr., Eva M. Hyatt, and Richard G. Starr Jr., "The Effects of Food Color on Perceived Flavor," *Journal of Marketing Theory and Practice* 8 (fall 2000): 60.

10. Eben Shapiro, "It's a Transparent Attempt to Revive Pepsi Cola's Sales," *New York Times*, April 13, 1992, http://www.nytimes.com/1992/04/13/business/it-s-a-transparent-attempt-to-revive-pepsi-s-cola-sales.html.

11. Howard R. Moskowitz, "Taste and Food Technology: Acceptability, Aesthetics, and Preference," in *Handbook of Perception*, vol. 6A, *Tasting and Smelling*, ed. Edward C. Carterette (New York: Academic Press, 1978), 162.

12. Moskowitz, "Taste and Food Technology," 163.

13. Richard Dawkins, *The Selfish Gene* (New York: Oxford University Press, 2006), 192.

14. Daniel Dennett, "Dangerous Memes," TED.com, February 2002, http://www.ted.com/talks/dan_dennett_on_dangerous_memes.html.

Chapter 11

1. Suzy Hagstrom, "Burger King Brings Service to the Table," *Orlando Sentinel*, September 18, 1992, http://articles.orlandosentinel.com/1992-09-18/business/9209180082_1_burger-king-king-restaurants-table.

2. Irene Kraft, "Burger King Table Service Slows Fast-Food Pace," *Morning Call*, October 4, 1992, http://articles.mcall.com/1992-10-04/features/2894261_1_fast-food-dining-burger-king-offer-table.

3. George Ritzer, *The McDonaldization of Society* (Thousand Oaks, CA: Pine Forge Press, 2004), 1.

4. Ritzer, *The McDonaldization of Society*, 46.

5. Ritzer, *The McDonaldization of Society*, 66.

6. Ritzer, *The McDonaldization of Society*, 66.

7. Ritzer, *The McDonaldization of Society*, 86.

8. Ritzer, *The McDonaldization of Society*, 106.

9. Perhaps no social theorist has made this argument with quite as much contempt for the rational process than Zygmunt Bauman. Bauman argued that the rationality involved in Western civilization established the very conditions that allowed for the Nazi Holocaust to take place, recounting all four features of the rational process—for Ritzer, those of McDonaldization—as found within the Holocaust. In a rather grim fashion it was, after all, these features of rationality that not only made the Holocaust efficient, but also allowed for its practitioners and defenders to make the terrifying claim that what they were engaged in was somehow done in the name of progress. Although it may be difficult to make the connections between Bauman's argument bound to the extreme instances of genocide and the rather benign irrationalities of McDonaldization revealed in the paradigm of the fast-food industry, making this connection is important in understanding the concept of the irrationality of rational processes. See Zygmunt Bauman, *Modernity and the Holocaust* (Ithaca, NY: Cornell University Press, 2000).

10. Ritzer, *The McDonaldization of Society*, 134.

11. Allowing or offering wireless connection suggests that some restaurants not only welcome longer visits to their establishments, but also are willing to accommodate non-paying or infrequently paying guests. This, of course, changes the model of ushering customers in, profiting, feeding them, and sending them on their way.

12. Michael Cosgrove, "McDonald's France Is Successfully Testing Table Service," *Le Figaro*, April 2, 2011, http://plus.lefigaro.fr/note/mcdonalds-france-is-successfully-testing-table-service-20110204-393988.

13. Ritzer, *The McDonaldization of Society*, 20.

14. Chip Lebovitz, "Burger King Delivery: A New Front in the Fast Food Wars?" *Fortune*, December 5, 2012, http://fortune.com/2012/12/05/burger-king-delivery-a-new-front-in-the-fast-food-wars.

15. Burger King, "Delivery Areas," BKDelivers.com, 2014, https://bkdelivers.com/#!areas.

Chapter 12

1. Evan Morris, *From Altoids to Zima: The Surprising Stories Behind 125 Famous Brand Names* (New York: Fireside, 2004), 83.

2. Lawrence L. Garber Jr. and Eve M. Hyatt, "Color as a Tool for Visual Persuasion," in *Persuasive Imagery: A Consumer Response Perspective*, ed. Linda M. Scott and Rajeev Batra (Mahwah, NJ: Routledge, 2003), 313.

3. George Lazarus, "Malt Competition Clearly Mounting," *Chicago Tribune*, March 24, 1994, http://articles.chicagotribune.com/1994-03-24/business/9403240139_1_malt-based-zima-bartles-jaymes.

4. Frank Kelley Rich, "Dead End Drinks: The Rise and Fall of Three Iconic Failures," *Modern Drunkard* 55, http://www.drunkard.com/issues/55/55-dead-end-drinks.html.

5. "Company News: Miller Ends Test Marketing of Clear Beer," *New York Times*, October 1, 1993, http://www.nytimes.com/1993/10/01/business/company-news-miller -ends-test-marketing-of-clear-beer.html.

6. Brendan Koerner, "The Long, Slow, Torturous Death of Zima: Fourteen Years after its Death, Zima Is Finally at Peace," *Slate*, November 26, 2008, http://www.slate .com/articles/life/drink/2008/11/the_long_slow_torturous_death_of_zima.html.

7. Koerner, "The Long, Slow, Torturous Death of Zima."

8. Paul Kirchner, *Forgotten Fads and Fabulous Flops: An Amazing Collection of Goofy Stuff That Seemed Like a Good Idea at the Time* (Los Angeles: General Publishing, 1995), 25.

9. Kirchner, *Forgotten Fads and Fabulous Flops*, 222–23.

10. A number of respectable toilet companies have marketed female urinals, but none has succeeded in changing the standard look of modern bathrooms. A list of these innovations include American Standard's Sanistand, Crane's Hy-san, and Kohler's Hygia—the earliest major invention of this sort from the 1930s. See Kirchner's *Forgotten Fads and Fabulous Flops*, 222–25.

11. Candace West and Don Zimmerman, "Doing Gender," *Gender and Society* 1, no. 2 (June 1987): 125–51.

12. West and Zimmerman, "Doing Gender," 126.

13. "Bring Back Zima," The Petitions Site, April 17, 2014, http://www.thepetition site.com/1/bringbackzima.

Chapter 13

1. Although the WOW brand was appended to these products by Frito-Lay, a subsidiary of PepsiCo, other products not owned by PepsiCo, including Procter & Gamble's Pringles, also marketed products with Olestra in them.

2. Marion Nestle, *Food Politics: How the Food Industry Influences Nutrition and Health* (Berkeley: University of California Press, 2014), 340.

3. Nestle, *Food Politics*, 344.

4. "F.D.A Panel Backs the Fake Fat Olestra," *New York Times*, June 18, 1998, http:// www.nytimes.com/1998/06/18/us/fda-panel-backs-the-fake-fat-olestra.html.

5. Liz Krieger, "Love Those Chips!: One Woman's Olestra Saga Can Be a Lesson for Us All," *Health Day*, January 20, 2017, https://consumer.healthday.com/encyclopedia/ digestive-health-14/digestion-health-news-200/love-those-chips-644757.html.

6. Glenn Collins, "In a Test, Snacks Hit the Spot Despite Some Rumblings," *New York Times*, August 24, 1997, http://www.nytimes.com/1997/08/24/business/in-a-test- snacks-hit-the-spot-despite-some-rumblings.html.

7. Collins, "In a Test, Snacks Hit the Spot."

8. Dana Canedy, "Low Fat's Lowered Expectations: Procter & Gamble Overestimates America's Olestra Craving," *New York Times*, July 21, 1999, http://www

.nytimes.com/1999/07/21/business/low-fat-s-lowered-expectations-procter-gamble
-overestimates-america-s-olestra.html.

9. Krieger, "Love Those Chips!"

10. Center for Science in the Public Interest, "Frito Lay's Wow Chips Hit Hoosiers Hard: Hundreds Suffer Diarrhea, Cramps, and Incontinence," news release, March 19, 1997, https://web.archive.org/web/20040621112728/http://www.cspinet.org/new/indy319.html.

11. Although the actual release on the website reveals the names of these individuals, I have removed these identifiers, viewing the names as irrelevant to the testimonies.

12. Center for Science in the Public Interest, "Frito Lay's Wow Chips Hit Hoosiers Hard."

13. Chris Regal, "WOW Chips and a Product That Is Too Good to Be True," *Health Central*, June 6, 2013, https://www.healthcentral.com/article/wow-chips-and-a-product that-is-too-good-to-be-true.

14. Krieger, "Love Those Chips!"

15. Malcolm Gladwell, "The Trouble with Fries: Fast Food Is Killing Us, Can It Be Fixed?" *New Yorker*, March 5, 2001, http://www.newyorker.com/magazine/2001/03/05/ the-trouble-with-fries.

16. Rachel Feltman, "Those Gut-Wrenching Olestra Chips from the '90s Might Have Been Good for Us," *Quartz*, April 4, 2014, https://qz.com/197458/those-gu t-wrenching-olestra-chips-from-the-90s-might-have-been-good-for-us.

Chapter 14

1. Charles Mackay, *Extraordinary Popular Delusions and the Madness of Crowds* (New York: Barnes & Noble, 1989), 257–80.

2. Mackay, *Extraordinary Popular Delusions and the Madness of Crowds*, 89–97.

3. "The Millennium Bug," House of Commons Library Research Paper 98/72, quoted in John Quiggin, "The Y2K Scare: Causes, Costs and Cures," *Australian Journal of Public Administration* 64, no. 3 (2005): 47.

4. Kathleen Melymuka, "Y2K Problems Compounded by Panic, Viruses," CNN, October 14, 1999, http://us.cnn.com/TECH/9910/14/y2k.virus.idg/index.html.

5. Edward Tenner, "Chronologically Incorrect," *Wilson Quarterly* 22, no. 4 (autumn 1998): 28.

6. "UK Drive to Beat Y2K Panic," BBC News, June 8, 1999, http://news.bbc.co.uk/ 2/hi/uk_news/363761.stm.

7. "White House Seeks to Dispel Y2K Panic," *Los Angeles Times*, December 13, 1999, http://articles.latimes.com/1999/dec/13/news/mn-43438.

8. Martyn Williams, "Computer Problems Hit Three Nuclear Plants in Japan," CNN, January 3, 2000, http://archives.cnn.com/2000/TECH/computing/01/03/japan .nukes.y2k.idg.

9. "Minor Bug Problems Arise," BBC News, January 1, 2000, http://news.bbc .co.uk/2/hi/science/nature/586620.stm.

10. Stanley Cohen, *Folk Devils and Moral Panics: The Creation of the Mods and the Rockers* (London: MacGibbon & Kee, 1972), 11.

11. Erich Goode and Nachman Ben-Yehuda, *Moral Panics: The Social Construction of Deviance* (Malden, MA: Blackwell, 1994), 104.

12. Tomatsu Shibutani, *Improvised News: A Sociological Study of Rumor* (New York: Bobbs-Merrill, 1966), 17.

13. Michael Gordon and Judith Miller, "U.S. Says Hussein Intensifies Quest for A-Bomb Parts," *New York Times*, September 8, 2002.

14. Dick Cheney, interview, *Meet the Press*, NBC, September 8, 2002, https://www.leadingtowar.com/PDFsources_claims_aluminum/2002_09_08_NBC.pdf.

15. Ralph L. Rosnow, "Inside Rumor: A Personal Journey," *American Psychologist* 46, no. 5 (May 1991): 485.

16. Rosnow, "Inside Rumor," 486.

17. Rosnow, "Inside Rumor," 487.

18. Rosnow, "Inside Rumor," 487.

19. Rosnow, "Inside Rumor," 486.

20. Rosnow, "Inside Rumor," 488.

21. Matthew L. Wald, "FAA Faulted on Fixing Year 2000 Computer Glitch," *New York Times*, February 4, 1998, http://www.nytimes.com/1998/02/04/us/faa-faulted-on-fixing-year-2000-computer-glitch.html.

22. Melissa Wahl, "Worries over Y2K Bug a Waste, Bankers Stress," *Chicago Tribune*, July 25, 1999, http://articles.chicagotribune.com/1999-07-25/business/9907250112_1_pinnacle-bank-y2k-ellen-seidman.

23. Jay Romano, "Dealing with the Y2K Bug," *New York Times*, August 16, 1998, http://www.nytimes.com/1998/08/16/realestate/your-home-dealing-with-the-y2k-bug.html.

24. Rosnow, "Inside Rumor," 487.

25. Andrea Hoplight Tapia, "Techno-Armageddon: The Millennial Christian Response to Y2K," *Review of Religious Research* 43, no. 3 (2002): 276.

26. Rosnow, "Inside Rumor," 488.

27. Tapia, "Techno-Armageddon," 277.

28. Goode and Ben-Yehuda, *Moral Panics*, 106.

Chapter 15

1. "Blimp Crashes into Oakland Restaurant," ESPN, January 31, 2001, http://espn.go.com/moresports/news/2001/0110/1005983.html.

2. Bob Costas, *On the Record with Bob Costas*, HBO Sports, March 14, 2001, https://www.youtube.com/watch?v=qexcFvsPetY.

3. "XFL Post-Game Conference," NBC Sports, February 3, 2001, https://www.washingtonpost.com/archive/lifestyle/2001/03/07/the-football-league-that-bombed/a80d2a8e-55fd-4f6f-894e-3234d9521647/?utm_term=.ecfe4c9fba98.

4. Brian Stelter, "WWE's 'Smackdown' Is Moving to Cable TV," *New York Times*, April 13, 2010, http://www.nytimes.com/2010/04/14/business/media/14wrestle.html.

5. Robert K. Merton, *Social Theory and Social Structure* (New York: Free Press, 1968), 186–87.

6. Merton, *Social Theory and Social Structure*, 187.

7. Merton, *Social Theory and Social Structure*, 195.

8. Originally viewed on YouTube.com; these commercials have now been removed.

9. Originally viewed on YouTube.com; these commercials have now been removed.

10. "The Rock Cuts Promo at LA Game," YouTube, 2001, https://www.youtube.com/watch?v=7YNoqJK4H8s.

11. Tom FitzGerald, "Top of the Sixth," *San Francisco Gate*, February 15, 2001.

12. Costas, *On the Record with Bob Costas*, March 14, 2001.

Chapter 16

1. Sean Loughlin, "House Cafeterias Change Names for 'French' Fries and 'French' Toast: Move Reflects Anger over France's Stance on Iraq," CNN, March 12, 2003, http://edition.cnn.com/2003/ALLPOLITICS/03/11/sprj.irq.fries.

2. Lars Bevanger, "'McAfrika' Burger Not to Everyone's Taste," BBC News, August 26, 2006, http://news.bbc.co.uk/2/hi/europe/2217450.stm.

3. Andrew Osborne, "New McDonald's: The New McAfrika Burger (Don't Tell the 12M Starving)," *Guardian* (UK), August 24, 2002, http://www.guardian.co.uk/world/2002/aug/24/famine.andrewosborn.

4. Osborne, "New McDonald's."

5. Matt Haig, *Brand Failures: The Truth about the 100 Biggest Branding Mistakes of All Time* (London: Kogan Page, 2003), 28.

6. Osborne, "New McDonald's."

7. Ashley, "Hilarious: McDonald's Menu Items That Were a Bust," *MoreClaremore*, November 9, 2014, http://moreclaremore.com/2014/11/09/hilarious-mcdonalds-menu-items-that-were-a-bust.

8. Roland Barthes, *Elements of Semiology*, trans. A. Lavers and C. Smith (London: Jonathan Cape, 1964), 77.

9. Roland Barthes, *Mythologies* (New York: Farrar, Straus & Giroux, 1972), 58.

10. Barthes, *Mythologies*, 53.

11. Barthes, *Elements*, 106–7.

12. Marita Sturken and Lisa Cartwright, *Practices of Looking: An Introduction to Visual Culture* (New York: Oxford University Press, 2001), 40.

13. Henry A. Giroux, "Benetton's 'World without Borders': Buying Social Change," in *The Subversive Imagination: Artists, Society, and Social Responsibility*, ed. Carol Becker, http://www.csus.edu/indiv/o/obriene/art7/readings/benetton.htm.

14. Bevanger, "'McAfrika' Burger Not to Everyone's Taste."

Chapter 17

1. Donald Bell, "Zune HD Review: Zune HD," *C-Net*, last modified September 17, 2009, https://www.cnet.com/products/zune-hd/review.

2. John Cook, "Zach Galifianakis to President Obama: Why Would You Get the Guy Who Created the Zune to Make Your Web Site?" *GeekWire*, last modified March 11, 2014, https://www.geekwire.com/2014/zach-galifianakis-president-obama-get-guy -created-zune-make-web-site. Although the development of the Healthcare.gov website was led by former Microsoft employee Kurt Delbene, Cook confirmed that Delbene most likely had little, if anything at all, to do with creating the Zune.

3. Gwynne Watkins, "Forget the Walkman, Can 'Guardians of the Galaxy Vol. 2' Make the Zune Cool?" *Yahoo! Movies*, last modified May 11, 2017, https://www.yahoo .com/movies/can-guardians-galaxy-vol-2-finally-make-zune-cool-174550564.html.

4. Zach Seemayer, "EXCLUSIVE: Chris Pratt Tries to Figure out a Zune in Hilarious 'Guardians of the Galaxy Vol. 2' Deleted Scene," *Entertainment Tonight*, August 7, 2017, http://www.etonline.com/movies/223258_chris_pratt_tries_to_figure_out_a _zune_hilarious_guardians_of_the_galaxy_vol_2_deleted_scene.

5. Jay Jayson, "Microsoft Didn't Want the Zune in Guardians of the Galaxy Vol. 2," ComicBook.com, last modified May 15, 2017, http://comicbook.com/mar vel/2017/05/16/zune-guardians-of-the-galaxy-2.

6. Paul Miller, "Zune Revealed by FCC as 'Toshiba 1089,'" *Engadget*, last modified August 25, 2006, https://www.engadget.com/2006/08/25/fcc-reveals-toshiba-1089-and -its-looking-a-whole-lot-like-a.

7. Bell, "Zune HD Review."

8. Mike Elgan, "Zune: So You Want to Be an iPod Killer?" *Computerworld*, last modified November 27, 2006, https://www.computerworld.com.au/article/172604/ zune_want_an_ipod_killer.

9. Anil Dash, "The Problem Is, The Zune Is Brown," *Anil Dash: A Blog about Making Culture*, November 14, 2006, http://anildash.com/2006/11/brown-zune.html.

10. Dash, "The Problem Is, The Zune Is Brown."

11. Matt Rossoff, "Former Microsoft Zune Boss Explains Why It Flopped," *Business Insider*, May 11, 2013, http://www.businessinsider.com/robbie-bach-explains-why-the -zune-flopped-2012-5.

12. Rossoff, "Former Microsoft Zune Boss Explains Why It Flopped."

13. Farhad Manjoo, "The Flop That Saved Microsoft," *Slate*, last modified October 10, 2012, http://www.slate.com/articles/technology/technology/2012/10/microsoft _zune_how_one_of_the_biggest_flops_in_tech_history_helped_revive.html.

14. "Why Did the iPod Succeed While the Zune Failed?" Quora.com, 2012, https:// www.quora.com/Why-did-the-iPod-succeed-while-the-Zune-failed.

15. Quora, "Why Did the iPod Succeed While the Zune Failed?"

16. Quora, "Why Did the iPod Succeed While the Zune Failed?"

17. Dev Patnaik, "Hybrid Thinking," presentation in the *Sparking a Culture of Innovation* series at the Chautauqua Institution, Chautauqua, New York, August 16, 2011, http:// library.fora.tv/2011/08/16/Jump_Associates_CEO_Dev_Patnaik_Hybrid_Thinking.

Chapter 18

1. "Status of Google Wave," Google.com, 2012, https://support.google.com/answer /1083134?hl=en.

2. "Status of Google Wave."

3. John D. Sutter, "The Genius Brothers behind Google Wave," CNN, October 27, 2009, http://edition.cnn.com/2009/TECH/10/27/rasmussen.brothers.google.wave.

4. "Eric Schmidt on Google Wave's Death," YouTube, 2010, https://www.youtube.com/watch?v=FJ-jNaAxISk.

5. Pierre Bourdieu, *Distinction: A Social Critique of the Judgment of Taste* (New York: Routledge, 2010), 95.

6. Bourdieu, *Distinction*, 95.

7. Gina Trapani, "On Google Wave and 'Failed' Experiments," *SmarterWare*, August 5, 2010, http://smarterware.org/6499/on-google-wave-and-failed-experiments.

8. Adam Ostrow, "Google Wave Invite Selling for $70 on eBay," *Mashable*, September 30, 2009, http://mashable.com/2009/09/30/google-wave-invite.

Bibliography

Adler, Patricia, and Peter Adler. "Dynamics of Inclusion and Exclusion in Preadolescent Cliques." *Social Psychology Quarterly* 58, no. 3 (1995): 145–62.

American Psychiatric Association. "307.47 Nightmare Disorder (formerly Dream Anxiety Disorder)." In *Diagnostic and Statistical Manual of Mental Disorders*, 4th ed., text revision, 631–34. Arlington, VA: American Psychiatric Publishing, 2000.

"Andy Rooney Dead at 92." CBS News, November 5, 2011, http://www.cbsnews.com/news/andy-rooney-dead-at-92 (December 12, 2011).

Ashley. "Hilarious: McDonald's Menu Items that were a Bust." *MoreClaremore.* November 9, 2014, http://moreclaremore.com/2014/11/09/hilarious-mcdonalds-menu-items-that-were-a-bust (September 20, 2014).

Auslander, Philip. *Liveness: Performance in a Mediated Culture.* New York: Routledge, 2008.

Barnard, Malcom. *Approaches to Understanding Visual Culture.* New York: Palgrave, 2001.

Barthes, Roland. *Elements of Semiology.* Translated by A. Lavers and C. Smith. London: Jonathan Cape, 1964.

———. *Mythologies.* New York: Farrar, Straus & Giroux, 1972.

Baudrillard, Jean, *Simulacra and Simulation.* Translated by Sheila Faria Glaser. Ann Arbor: University of Michigan Press, 1994.

Bauman, Zygmunt. *Modernity and the Holocaust.* Ithaca, NY: Cornell University Press, 2000.

bdevore30. "The Laserdisc Failure: The First Optical Disc Format." Storyfy.com, 2016, https://storify.com/bdevore30/the-laserdisc-failure-57ba652f10948ce140a48dd8 (18 October 18, 2017).

Beastie Boys. "Mullet Head." *Ill Communication.* Grand Royal Records, 1994, compact disc.

Becker, Howard S. *Outsiders: Studies in the Sociology of Deviance.* New York: Macmillan, 1963.

Bell, Donald. "Zune HD Review: Zune HD." *C-Net,* last modified September 17, 2009, https://www.cnet.com/products/zune-hd/review (May 28, 2017).

Berger, James. *After the End: Representations of Post-Apocalypse.* Minneapolis: University of Minnesota Press, 1999.

Berger, John. *Ways of Seeing.* London: Penguin, 2008.

Bernard, James. "Why the World Is after Vanilla Ice." *New York Times,* February 3, 1991, http://www.nytimes.com/1991/02/03/arts/why-the-world-is-after-vanilla-ice .html (June 22, 2012).

———. "Mind Blowin'." *Entertainment Weekly,* March 25, 1994, http://www.ew.com/ ew/article/0,,301550,00.html (June 19, 2012).

Best, Joel. *Flavor of the Month: Why Smart People Fall for Fads.* Berkeley: University of California Press, 2006.

Best Worst Movie. Directed by Michael Stephenson. 2009; New York: New Video, 2010. DVD.

Bevanger, Lars. "'McAfrika' Burger Not to Everyone's Taste." BBC News, August 26, 2006, http://news.bbc.co.uk/2/hi/europe/2217450.stm (March 19, 2014).

Blackhall, Sue. *The World's Greatest Blunder.* London: Octopus Books, 1997.

Blackman, Melinda C., and Collen A. Kvoska. *Nutrition Psychology: Improving Dietary Adherence.* Sudbury, MA: Jones and Bartlett, 1992.

"Blimp Crashes into Oakland Restaurant." ESPN, January 31, 2001, http://espn .go.com/moresports/news/2001/0110/1005983.html (December 2, 2015).

"BluBlocker® Sunglasses Get a Special Invite to the Latin Grammy Awards." *Yahoo! Finance,* November 15, 2012, http://finance.yahoo.com/news/blublocker-sunglasses -very-special-invite-213800501.html (December 30, 2012).

"Blue Light Has a Dark Side." *Harvard Health Letter,* May 2012, http://www.health.har vard.edu/newsletters/Harvard_Health_Letter/2012/May/blue-light-has-a-dark-side# (January 19, 2013).

Bonsall, Thomas A. *Disaster in Dearborn: The Story of the Edsel.* Palo Alto, CA: Stanford University Press, 2002.

Bourdieu, Pierre. *Distinction: A Social Critique of the Judgment of Taste.* New York: Routledge, 2010.

Brin, David. "The Postman: The Movie and the Book." YouTube, October 30, 2012, https://www.youtube.com/watch?v=IgWH0BTaOMg (December 14, 2014).

"Bring Back Zima," The Petitions Site, April 17 2014, http://www.thepetitionsite .com/1/bringbackzima (June 9, 2015).

Bryant, Adam. "Coke Adds a New Cola to Its 'New Age' Stable." *New York Times,* December 15, 1992, http://www.nytimes.com/1992/12/15/business/company-news -coke-adds-a-clear-cola-to-its-new-age-stable.html (December 9, 2013).

Bryne, John A. *Whiz Kids: The Founding Fathers of American Business and the Legacy They Left Us.* New York: Doubleday, 1993.

Burger King, "Delivery Areas." BKDelivers.com, accessed December 16, 2014, https:// bkdelivers.com/#!areas.

Cabral, Luis, and David Backus. "Betamax and VHS," Firms and Markets Mini Case. New York University, Leonard N. Stern School of Business, 2002, http://pages.stern .nyu.edu/~lcabral/teaching/betamax.pdf (September 20, 2014).

Caruth, Cathy. *Trauma: Explorations in Memory.* Baltimore: Johns Hopkins University Press, 1995.

Canedy, Dana. "Low Fat's Lowered Expectations: Procter & Gamble Overestimates America's Olestra Craving." *New York Times*, July 21, 1999, http://www.nytimes .com/1999/07/21/business/low-fat-s-lowered-expectations-procter-gamble-overesti mates-america-s-olestra.html (February 24, 2017).

Center for Science in the Public Interest. "Frito Lay's Wow Chips Hit Hoosiers Hard: Hundreds Suffer Diarrhea, Cramps, and Incontinence." News release, March 19, 1997, https://web.archive.org/web/20040621112728/http://www.cspinet.org/new/ indy319.html (June 22, 2017).

Cheney, Dick. Interview. *Meet the Press*. NBC, September 8, 2002, https://www.leading towar.com/PDFsources_claims_aluminum/2002_09_08_NBC.pdf.

Cobb, James C. "What We Can Learn from Coca-Cola's Biggest Blunder." *Time*, July 10, 2015, http://time.com/3950205/new-coke-history-america (December 13, 2017).

Cohen, Stanley. *Folk Devils and Moral Panics: The Creation of the Mods and the Rockers.* London: MacGibbon & Kee, 1972.

Collins, Glenn. "In a Test, Snacks Hit the Spot Despite Some Rumblings." *New York Times*, August 24, 1997, http://www.nytimes.com/1997/08/24/business/in-a-test -snacks-hit-the-spot-despite-some-rumblings.html (June 22, 2017).

"Company News; Miller Ends Test Marketing of Clear Beer." *New York Times*, October 1, 1993, http://www.nytimes.com/1993/10/01/business/company-news-miller-ends-test -marketing-of-clear-beer.html (May 12, 2014).

Conklin, Mike. "Start the Presses, the First Cubs Book Has Been Announced . . ." *Chicago Tribune*, October 17, 1989, http://articles.chicagotribune.com/1989–10–17/ sports/8901230412_1_cubs-big-easy-lineup (June 12, 2013).

Cook, John. "Zach Galifianakis to President Obama: Why Would You Get the Guy Who Created the Zune to Make Your Web Site?" *GeekWire*, last modified March 11, 2014, https://www.geekwire.com/2014/zach-galifianakis-president-obama-get-guy -created-zune-make-web-site (June 12, 2017).

"Coors Enters Bottled Water Market." *New York Times*, January 16, 1990, http://www .nytimes.com/1990/01/16/business/coors-enters-bottled-water-market.html (June 12, 2012).

Cosgrove, Michael. "McDonald's France Is Successfully Testing Table Service." *Le Figaro*, April 2, 2011, http://plus.lefigaro.fr/note/mcdonalds-france-is-successfully -testing-table-service-20110204–393988 (September 12, 2011).

Costas, Bob. *On the Record with Bob Costas*. HBO Sports, March 16, 2002, https://www .youtube.com/watch?v=qexcFvsPetY (February 7, 2018).

Curtis, Jason. "LaserDisc (1983–2001)." Museum of Obsolete Media, March 14, 2009, http://www.obsoletemedia.org/laserdisc (January 19, 2017).

Cusumano, Michael, Yiorgos Mylonadis, and Richard Rosenbloom. "Strategic Maneu-vering and Mass-Market Dynamic: The Triumph of VHS over Beta." *Business History Review* 66 (1992): 51–94.

Cyrus, Billy Ray. "I Want My Mullet Back." *Wanna Be Your Joe*. New Door Records UM, 2006, compact disc.

Dash, Anil. "The Problem Is, The Zune Is Brown." *Anil Dash: A Blog about Making Culture*, November 14, 2006, http://anildash.com/2006/11/brown-zune.html (June 12, 2017).

Davis, Fred. *Fashion, Culture, and Identity.* Chicago: University of Chicago Press, 1992.

Dawkins, Richard. *The Selfish Gene.* New York: Oxford University Press, 2006.

Demott, John S. "All Afizz over the New Coke." *Time,* June 24, 1985, http://content .time.com/time/magazine/article/0,9171,959449,00.html (December 14, 2017).

Dennett, Daniel. "Dangerous Memes." TED.com, February 2002, http://www.ted.com/ talks/dan_dennett_on_dangerous_memes.html (December 12, 2012).

Dicke, Tom. "The Edsel: Forty Years as a Symbol of Failure." *Journal of Popular Culture* 43, no. 3 (2010): 486–502.

Dorfman, Ariel. *The Empire's Old Clothes: What the Lone Ranger, Babar and other Innocent Heroes Do to Our Minds.* New York: Pantheon, 1983.

Dörner, Dietrich. *The Logic of Failure: Recognizing and Avoiding Error in Complex Situations.* New York: Basic Books, 1996.

Douglas, Mary. *Purity and Danger: An Analysis of Concepts of Pollution and Taboo.* New York: Routledge, 1966.

Dussenbury, Phil. *Then We Set His Hair on Fire: Insights and Accidents from a Hall-of-Fame Career in Advertising.* New York: Penguin, 2005.

Eagleton, Terry. *The Idea of Culture.* Malden, MA: Blackwell, 2000.

Elgan, Mike. "Zune: So You Want to Be an iPod Killer?" *Computerworld,* last modified November 27, 2006, https://www.computerworld.com.au/article/172604/zune_ want_an_ipod_killer (June 20, 2017).

Ellen, Pam Scholder, and Paula Fitzgerald Bone. "Stained by the Label: Stigma and the Case of Genetically Modified Foods." *Journal of Public Policy & Marketing* 27, no. 1 (2008): 69–82.

Epstein, Dan. *Big Hair and Plastic Grass: A Funky Ride through Baseball and America in the Swinging '70s.* New York: Thomas Dunne Books, 2010.

"Eric Schmidt on Google Wave's Death." YouTube, 2010, https://www.youtube.com/ watch?v=FJ-jNaAxISk (December 1, 2014).

Ewen, Stuart. *All Consuming Images: The Politics of Style in Contemporary Culture.* New York: Basic Books, 1988.

———. *Captains of Consciousness: Advertising and the Social Roots of Consumer Culture.* New York: Basic Books, 2001.

Ewen, Stuart, and Elizabeth Ewen. *Channels of Desire: Mass Images and the Shaping of American Consciousness.* New York: McGraw-Hill, 1982.

Ewens, Sophie. "Where to Buy Richie Tenenbaum Sunglasses." *IT News Online,* 2012, http://itonlinenews.com/where-to-buy-richie-tenenbaum-sunglasses (December 12, 2013).

"F.D.A. Panel Backs the Fake Fat Olestra." *New York Times,* June 18, 1998, http://www nytimes.com/1998/06/18/us/fda-panel-backs-the-fake-fat-olestra.html (February 20, 2017).

Feel Good about Failure: The Dark Side of Self-Esteem Classes. 1999; Princeton, NJ: Films for the Humanities & Sciences, 2003. DVD.

Feltman, Rachel. "Those Gut-Wrenching Olestra Chips from the '90s Might Have Been Good for Us." *Quartz,* April 4, 2014, https://qz.com/197458/those-gut-wrenching -olestra-chips-from-the-90s-might-have-been-good-for-us/ (June 23, 2017).

FitzGerald, Tom. "Top of the Sixth." *San Francisco Gate,* February 15, 2001.

Fizz or Fizzle? 1992; New Hudson, MI: ABC News Productions, 2007. DVD.

Flaim, Kate Bonamici. "The Education of an Accidental CEO: Lessons Learned from the Trailer Park to the Corner Office." *Fast Company*, October 1, 2007, http://www .fastcompany.com/60555/winging-it (June 13, 2013).

Frank, Thomas. *The Conquest of Cool: Business Culture, Counterculture, and the Rise of Hip Consumerism.* Chicago: University of Chicago Press, 1997.

Garber, Lawrence L. Jr., and Eve M. Hyatt. "Color as a Tool for Visual Persuasion." In *Persuasive Imagery: A Consumer Response Perspective*, ed. Linda M. Scott and Rajeev Batra, 313–36. Mahwah, NJ: Routledge, 2003.

Garber, Lawrence L. Jr., Eva M. Hyatt, and Richard G. Starr Jr. "The Effects of Food Color on Perceived Flavor." *Journal of Marketing Theory and Practice* 8 (fall 2000): 59–72.

Garfield, Bob. "Why Make Bud Dry an Antidote to Life's Problems? Don't Ask." *Advertising Age*, October 1, 1990, 58.

Gentilviso, Chris. "Blublocker Sunglasses." *Time*, August, 18, 2010, http://www.time .com/time/specials/packages/article/0,28804,2011470_2011194_2011181,00.html (January 18, 2014).

Gibron, Bill. "Waterworld (1995): Blu-ray." *PopMatters.* October 21, 2009, http://www. popmatters.com/pm/post/114985-waterworld-1995-blu-ray/ (December 22, 2013).

Giroux, Henry A. "Benetton's 'World without Borders': Buying Social Change." In *The Subversive Imagination: Artists, Society, and Social Responsibility*, ed. Carol Becker, 187–207. New York: Routledge, 1994. http://www.csus.edu/indiv/o/obriene/art7/ readings/benetton.htm (January 19, 2013).

Giuliani, Rudy. Interview by John Gambling, *John Gambling Show*, WABC, September 21, 2001. http://transcripts.cnn.com/TRANSCRIPTS/0109/21/se.20.html (December 23, 2012).

Gladwell, Malcolm. "The Trouble with Fries: Fast Food Is Killing Us, Can It Be Fixed?" *New Yorker*, March 5, 2001, http://www.newyorker.com/magazine/2001/03/05/the -trouble-with-fries (June 28, 2017).

Glass, Robert L. *Software Runaways: Lessons Learned from Massive Software Project Failures.* Upper Saddle River, NJ: Prentice Hall, 1998.

———. *Computing Calamities: Lessons Learned from Products, Projects, and Companies that Failed.* Upper Saddle River, NJ: Prentice Hall, 1999.

Glitter. Directed by Vondie Curtis-Hall. 2001; Culver City, CA: Sony Pictures Home Entertainment, 2002. DVD.

"Glitter." Rotten Tomatoes. http://www.rottentomatoes.com/m/glitter (December 12, 2014).

Goffman, Erving. *The Presentation of Self in Everyday Life.* Garden City, NY: Doubleday Anchor Books, 1959.

Goode, Erich, and Nachman Ben-Yehuda. *Moral Panics: The Social Construction of Deviance.* Malden, MA: Blackwell, 1994.

Gordon, Michael, and Judith Miller. "U.S. Says Hussein Intensifies Quest for A-Bomb Parts." *New York Times*, September 8, 2002.

Gorman, Ryan, and Skye Gould. "This Mistake from 30 Years Ago Almost Destroyed Coca-Cola." *Business Insider*, April 23, 2015, http://www.businessinsider.com/new-coke -the-30th-anniversary-of-coca-colas-biggest-mistake-2015–4 (December 13, 2017).

Gould, Brian. "Consumer Board's Consumer Confidence Index, 1977–2015." University of Wisconsin–Madison, Agricultural and Applied Economics. http://future.aae .wisc.edu/data/monthly_values/by_area/998?grid=true (September 9, 2015).

Grossberg, Lawrence, Cary Nelson, and Paula Treichler, eds. *Cultural Studies*. New York: Routledge, 1992.

Hagstrom, Suzy. "Burger King Brings Service to the Table." *Orlando Sentinel*, September 18, 1992, http://articles.orlandosentinel.com/1992–09–18/business/9209180082_1_ burger-king-king-restaurants-table (September 19, 2012).

Haig, Matt. *Brand Failures: The Truth about the 100 Biggest Branding Mistakes of All Time*. London: Kogan Page, 2003.

Hall, Stuart, ed. *Representation: Cultural Representations and Signifying Practices*. Thousand Oaks, CA: Sage, 2011.

———. "Encoding, Decoding." In *The Cultural Studies Reader*, ed. Simon During, 507–17. London: Routledge, 1999.

Hammidi, Tania, and Susan B. Kaiser. "Doing Beauty: Negotiating Lesbian Looks in Everyday Life." In *Lesbians, Levis and Lipstick: The Meaning of Beauty in Our Lives*, ed. Jeanine C. Cogan and Joanie M. Erikson, 55–63. New York: Harrington Park Press, 1999.

Haoues, Rachid. "30 Years Ago Today, Coca-Cola Made Its Worst Mistake." CBS News, April 23, 2015, https://www.cbsnews.com/news/30-years-ago-today-coca-cola -new-coke-failure (December 13, 2017).

Hartford, Tim. *Adapt: Why Success Always Starts with Failure*. New York: Farrar, Straus & Giroux, 2011.

Heaven's Gate. Directed by Michael Cimino. 1980; Beverly Hills, CA: MGM Studios, 2000. DVD.

"Here's to Gay Mullins, Who Gave His All for the Real Thing—but Hey, Gay, Why Stop with Coke?" *People*, July 29, 1985, http://people.com/archive/heres-to-gay-mull ins-who-gave-his-all-for-the-real-thing-but-hey-gay-why-stop-with-coke-vol-24-no-5/ (December 14, 2017).

Henderson, Alan. *Mullet Madness! The Haircut That's Business Up Front and a Party in the Back*. New York: Skyhorse, 2007.

"History." BluBlocker, http://www.blublocker.com/pages/history (June 19, 2013).

Hoffman, Frank, and Bill Bailey. *Arts & Entertainment Fads*. Binghamton, NY: Harrington Park Press, 1990.

Honan, Matthew. "The Best: Obsolete Technologies from the Sundial to the Laser Disc." *Wired*, October 23, 2007, https://www.wired.com/2007/10/st-best-20/ (January 9, 2017).

Howard the Duck. Directed by Willard Huyk. 1986; Hollywood, CA: Universal Studios, 2009. DVD.

Hunt, Dennis. "To Rent or Buy Laser Discs? That Is the Question." *Los Angeles Times*, August 16, 1991, http://articles.latimes.com/1991-08-16/entertainment/ca-590_1_ laser-discs (June 11, 2017).

Itzkoff, Dave. "That Film May Be Trash, but You Can Still Recycle It." *New York Times*, May 13, 2010, http://www.nytimes.com/2010/05/13/movies/13worst.html?_r=0 (May 12, 2012).

Jancelewicz, Chris. "Vanilla Ice on 'Canada Sings' and Why It's Anything but Another 'Idol.'" *AOL TV*, August 2, 2011, http://www.aoltv.com/2011/08/02/vanilla-ice -canada-sings-interview (June 22, 2012).

Jayson, Jay. "Microsoft Didn't Want the Zune in *Guardians of the Galaxy Vol. 2*." ComicBook.com, last modified May 15, 2017, http://comicbook.com/marvel/2017/05/16/ zune-guardians-of-the-galaxy-2 (June 2, 2017).

Johnson, Richard A. *American Fads: From Silly Putty and Swallowing Goldfish to Hot Pants and Hula Hoops, Forty Crazes that Swept the Nation.* New York: Beech Tree Books, 1985.

Karabell, Zachary. "Al Qaeda's Failure on Wall Street." *Daily Beast*, September 11, 2011, http://www.thedailybeast.com/articles/2011/09/09/9-11-anniversary-al-qaeda-s -failure-on-wall-street-vertical.html (March 15, 2012).

Karger, Dave. "Vanilla Ice Cracks." *Entertainment Weekly*, May 14, 1999, http://www .ew.com/ew/article/0,,273353,00.html (June 20, 2012).

Kehr, Dave. "Goodbye, DVD. Hello Future." *New York Times*, March 4, 2011, http:// www.nytimes.com/2011/03/06/movies/homevideo/06dvds.html (September 13, 2017).

Kirchner, Paul. *Forgotten Fads and Fabulous Flops: An Amazing Collection of Goofy Stuff That Seemed Like a Good Idea at the Time.* Los Angeles: General Publishing, 1995.

Koerner, Brendan. "The Long, Slow, Torturous Death of Zima: Fourteen Years after its Death, Zima Is Finally at Peace." *Slate*, November 26, 2008, http://www.slate.com/ articles/life/drink/2008/11/the_long_slow_torturous_death_of_zima.html (May 17, 2012).

Kraft, Irene "Burger King Table Service Slows Fast-Food Pace." *Morning Call*, October 4, 1992, http://articles.mcall.com/1992-10-04/features/2894261_1_fast-food-dining -burger-king-offer-table (September 11, 2012).

Krieger, Liz. "Love Those Chips! One Woman's Olestra Saga Can Be a Lesson for Us All." *Health Day*, January 20, 2017, https://consumer.healthday.com/encyclopedia/ digestive-health-14/digestion-health-news-200/love-those-chips-644757.html (February 25, 2017).

Kurzman, Charles, Chelise Anderson, Clinton Key, Youn Ok Lee, Mairead Moloney, Alexis Silver, and Maria W. Van Ryn. "Celebrity Status." *Sociological Theory* 25, no. 4 (2007): 347–67.

Larson, Mark, and Barney Hoskyns. *The Mullet: Hairstyle of the Gods.* New York: Bloomsbury, 1999.

Lazarus, George. "Malt Competition Clearly Mounting." *Chicago Tribune*, March 24, 1994, http://articles.chicagotribune.com/1994-03-24/business/9403240139_1_malt -based-zima-bartles-jaymes (June 9, 2015).

Lebovitz, Chip. "Burger King Delivery: A New Front in the Fast Food Wars?" *Fortune*, December 5, 2012, http://fortune.com/2012/12/05/burger-king-delivery-a-new -front-in-the-fast-food-wars (September 8, 2011).

Lebow, Victor. "Price Competition in 1955." *Journal of Retailing* (spring 1955), http:// www.gcafh.org/edlab/Lebow.pdf (December 12, 2012).

Licata, Elizabeth. "Meet 12 Celebs Who Pull Off Harem Pants So Well That You'll Actually Buy a Pair." *Gloss*, May 12, 2014, http://www.thegloss.com/2014/05/16/ fashion/celebrities-harem-pants-how-to-wear-them (June 18, 2014).

Locher, David A. "The Industrial Identity Crisis: The Failure of a Newly Forming Subculture to Identify Itself." In *Youth Culture: Identity in a Postmodern World*, ed. Jonathon S. Epstein, 100–117. Malden, MA: Blackwell, 1998.

Loughlin, Sean. "House Cafeterias Change Names for 'French' Fries and 'French' Toast: Move Reflects Anger over France's Stance on Iraq." CNN, March 12, 2003, http://edition.cnn.com/2003/ALLPOLITICS/03/11/sprj.irq.fries (May 15, 2014).

Mackay, Charles. *Extraordinary Popular Delusions and the Madness of Crowds*. New York: Barnes & Noble, 1989.

Manjoo, Farhad. "The Flop That Saved Microsoft." *Slate*, last modified October 10, 2012, http://www.slate.com/articles/technology/technology/2012/10/microsoft_zune_how_one_of_the_biggest_flops_in_tech_history_helped_revive.html (June 6, 2017).

Marcuse, Herbert. "Liberation from the Affluent Society." In *The Dialectics of Liberation*, ed. David Cooper, 175–92. Baltimore: Penguin, 1968.

"Mariah Blames 9/11 for Glitter Flop." *Independent* (Ireland), January 25, 2010, http://www.independent.ie/entertainment/movies/mariah-blames-911-for-glitter-flop-26625900.html (June 11, 2012).

Marum, Andrew, and Frank Parise. *Follies and Foibles: A View of 20th Century Fads*. New York: Facts on File, 1984.

Maslin, Jane. "Film Review: *Waterworld*; Aquatic Armageddon with Plenty of Toys." *New York Times*, July 28, 1995, http://movies.nytimes.com/movie/review?res=990CE1DD143BF93BA15754C0A963958260 (December 19, 2013).

McGill, Douglas C. "'Smokeless' Cigarette's Hapless Start." *New York Times*, November 19, 1988.

McLachlan, Megan. "10 Awesome Sunglasses Inspired by Movies." *Primer*, 2011, http://www.primermagazine.com/2011/spend/10-awesome-sunglasses-inspired-by-movies (December 12, 2012).

MC Hammer 2 Legit: The Videos. Directed by Rupert Wainwright. New York: Capitol Records, 2002. DVD.

Melymuka, Kathleen. "Y2K Problems Compounded by Panic, Viruses." CNN, October 14, 1999, https://us.cnn.com/TECH/computing/9910/14/y2k.virus.idg/index.html (December 2, 2014).

Merton, Robert K. *Social Theory and Social Structure*. New York: Free Press, 1968.

Meyer, Carla. "'Glitter' Reveals Carey Can Pose, but Not Act." *San Francisco Gate*, September 22, 2001, http://www.sfgate.com/movies/article/Glitter-reveals-Carey-can-pose-but-not-act-2876827.php (December 14, 2013).

"The Millennium Bug." House of Commons Library Research Paper 98/72. Quoted in John Quiggin, "The Y2K Scare: Causes, Costs and Cures." *Australian Journal of Public Administration* 64, no. 3 (2005): 46–55.

Miller, Paul. "Zune Revealed by FCC as 'Toshiba 1089.'" *Engadget*, last modified August 25, 2006, https://www.engadget.com/2006/08/25/fcc-reveals-toshiba-1089-and-its-looking-a-whole-lot-like-a/ (June 1, 2017).

"Minor Bug Problems Arise." BBC News, January 1, 2000, http://news.bbc.co.uk/2/hi/science/nature/586620.stm (January 12, 2013).

Molotch, Harvey. *Where Stuff Comes From: How Toasters, Toilets, Cars, Computers and Many Other Things Come to Be as They Are*. New York: Routledge, 2003.

Morris, Evan. *From Altoids to Zima: The Surprising Stories Behind 125 Famous Brand Names.* New York: Fireside, 2004.

Moskowitz, Howard R. "Taste and Food Technology: Acceptability, Aesthetics, and Preference." In *Handbook of Perception.* Vol. 6A, *Tasting and Smelling,* ed. Edward C. Carterette, 157–92. New York: Academic Press, 1978.

Nestle, Marion. *Food Politics: How the Food Industry Influences Nutrition and Health.* Berkeley: University of California Press, 2014.

"1996 Means Kentucky, Converse and Those Denim Unis." *Lost Lettermen,* 1996, http://www.lostlettermen.com/lost-uniforms-1996-means-kentucky-converse-and -those-denim-unis (December 5, 2014).

Osborne, Andrew. "New McDonald's: The New McAfrika Burger (Don't Tell the 12M Starving)." *Guardian* (UK), August 24, 2002, http://www.guardian.co.uk/ world/2002/aug/24/famine.andrewosborn (April 19, 2012).

Ostrow, Adam. "Google Wave Invite Selling for $70 on eBay." *Mashable,* September 30, 2009, http://mashable.com/2009/09/30/google-wave-invite/ (December 9, 2014).

Pantini, Charles. *Pantini's Parade of Fads, Follies and Manias: The Origins of Our Most Cherished Obsessions.* New York: Harper Perennial, 1991.

Patniak, Dev. "Hybrid Thinking." Presentation in the *Sparking a Culture of Innovation* series at the Chautauqua Institution, Chautauqua, New York, August 16, 2011. http:// library.fora.tv/2011/08/16/Jump_Associates_CEO_Dev_Patnaik_Hybrid_Thinking (June 5, 2017).

Pendergrast, Mark. *For God, Country, and Coca-Cola: The Definitive History of the Great American Soft Drink and the Company That Makes It.* New York: Basic Books, 2004.

"Pepsi Will Market-Test a Clear-Colored Cola: Retailing: It Could Expand the $46-Billion Soft Drink Market, Analysts Say." *Los Angeles Times,* April 13, 1992, http:// articles.latimes.com/1992–04–13/business/fi-244_1_soft-drink (June 12, 2013).

Perrow, Charles. *Normal Accidents: Living with High-Risk Technologies.* Princeton, NJ: Princeton University Press, 1999.

Postman. Directed by Kevin Costner. 1997; Burbank, CA: Warner Home Video, 1998. DVD.

Puig, Claudie. "Despite Mariah's Pipes, Glitter Is Definitely Not Gold." *USA Today,* September 20, 2001, http://usatoday30.usatoday.com/life/enter/movies/2001-09-21 -glitter.htm (December 12, 2012).

"The Real Story of New Coke." *Coca-Cola Journey.* November 14, 2012, http://www .coca-colacompany.com/stories/coke-lore-new-coke (December 14, 2017).

Regal, Chris. "WOW Chips and a Product That Is Too Good to Be True." *HealthCentral,* June 6, 2013, https://www.healthcentral.com/article/wow-chips-and-a-product -that-is-too-good-to-be-true (June 22, 2017).

Rich, Frank Kelley. "Dead End Drinks: The Rise and Fall of Three Iconic Failures." *Modern Drunkard* 55, http://www.drunkard.com/issues/55/55-dead-end-drinks.html (April 19, 2016).

Ritzer, George. *Classical Sociological Theory.* New York: McGraw-Hill, 2000.

———. *The Mcdonaldization of Society.* Thousand Oaks, CA: Pine Forge Press, 2004.

"The Rock Cuts Promo at LA Game." YouTube, 2001, https://www.youtube.com/ watch?v=7YNoqJK4H8s (June 12, 2015).

Romano, Jay. "Dealing with the Y2K Bug." *New York Times*, August 16, 1998, http://www.nytimes.com/1998/08/16/realestate/your-home-dealing-with-the-y2k-bug.html (February 15, 2013).

Ronson, Jon. "Psycho Dabble." *This American Life*, July 10, 2009. Podcast audio. https://www.thisamericanlife.org/385/pro-se/act-one-0 (February 14, 2011).

Rose, Gillian. *Visual Methodologies: An Introduction to Researching with Visual Materials.* Thousand Oaks, CA: Sage, 2012.

Rosnow, Ralph L. "Inside Rumor: A Personal Journey." *American Psychologist* 46, no. 5 (May 1991): 484–96.

Rossoff, Matt. "Former Microsoft Zune Boss Explains Why It Flopped." *Business Insider*, May 11, 2013, http://www.businessinsider.com/robbie-bach-explains-why-the-zune -flopped-2012-5 (December 12, 2015).

Rowley, Ian. "Next-Gen DVD's Porn Struggle." *Bloomberg Businessweek*, January 22, 2007. http://www.businessweek.com/stories/2007-01-22/next-gen-dvds-porn-strug glebusinessweek-business-news-stock-market-and-financial-advice (October 9, 2014).

Sandage, Scott A. *Born Losers: A History of Failure in America.* Cambridge, MA: Harvard University Press, 2005.

Schindler, Robert M. "The Real Lesson of New Coke: The Value of Focus Groups for Predicting the Effects of Social Influence." *Marketing Research*, December 1992, 23–27.

Schorb, Jodi R., and Tania N. Hammidi. "Sho-Lo Showdown: The Do's and Don'ts of Lesbian Chic." *Tulsa Studies in Women's Literature* 19, no. 2 (2000): 255–68.

Seemayer, Zach. "EXCLUSIVE: Chris Pratt Tries to Figure out a Zune in Hilarious 'Guardians of the Galaxy Vol. 2' Deleted Scene." *Entertainment Tonight*, August 7, 2017, http://www.etonline.com/movies/223258_chris_pratt_tries_to_figure_out_a _zune_hilarious_guardians_of_the_galaxy_vol_2_deleted_scene (June 5, 2017).

Shapiro, Eben. "It's a Transparent Attempt to Revive Pepsi Cola's Sales." *New York Times*, April 13, 1992, http://www.nytimes.com/1992/04/13/business/it-s-a-transpar ent-attempt-to-revive-pepsi-s-cola-sales.html (June 12, 2012).

Shibutani, Tomatsu. *Improvised News: A Sociological Study of Rumor.* New York: Bobbs-Merrill, 1966.

Simmel, Georg. "Fashion," *American Journal of Sociology* 62, no. 6 (May 1956): 541–58.

Smith, Martin J., and Patrick J. Kiger. *Poplorica: A Popular History of the Fads, Mavericks, Inventions, and Lore That Shaped Modern America.* New York: HarperResource, 2004.

Sorensen, Erin. "Longhorns Practice Uniforms Are Almost as Bad as Auburn's." *Bleacher Report*, August 6, 2012, http://bleacherreport.com/articles/1287054-texas-football -longhorns-practice-uniforms-are-almost-as-bad-as-auburns (December 20, 2014).

Stack, Peter. "Insufficient 'Postman:' Costner's Post-Apocalyptic Saga Long and Bland." *San Francisco Gate*, December 25 1997, http://www.sfgate.com/movies/article/FILM -REVIEW-Insufficient-Postman-Costner-s-2788146.php#ixzz2HGwSsHBl (December 15, 2013).

"Status of Google Wave." Google.com, 2012, https://support.google.com/ answer/1083134?hl=en (December 12, 2014).

Stearn, Gerald Emanuel, ed. *McLuhan: Hot & Cool, A Critical Symposium.* New York: Dial, 1967.

Steinberg, Neil. *Hatless Jack: The President, the Fedora, and the History of an American Style.* New York: Plume, 2004.

Stelter, Brian. "WWE's 'Smackdown' Is Moving to Cable TV." *New York Times,* April 13, 2010, http://www.nytimes.com/2010/04/14/business/media/14wrestle.html.

Storey, John. *An Introduction to Cultural Theory and Popular Culture.* Athens: University of Georgia Press, 1998.

The Story of Stuff. Written by Annie Leonard, Louis Fox, and Jonah Sachs; directed by Louis Fox. Washington, DC: Free Range Studios, 2007. http://storyofstuff.org/mov ies/story-of-stuff (December 17, 2012).

Strom, Stephanie. "Donald R. Keough, Who Led Coca-Cola through New Coke Debacle, Dies at 88." *New York Times,* February 25, 2015, https://www.nytimes .com/2015/02/25/business/donald-r-keough-who-led-coca-cola-through-new-coke -debacle-dies-at-88.html (December 13, 2017).

Sturken, Marita, and Lisa Cartwright. *Practices of Looking: An Introduction to Visual Culture.* New York: Oxford University Press, 2001.

Sudo, Chuck. "The Chicagoist Flashback: The White Sox Don Shorts for the First Time." *Chicagoist,* August 8, 2012, http://chicagoist.com/2012/08/08/the_chicago ist_flashback_the_white.php (September 20, 2014).

Sutter, John D. "The Genius Brothers behind Google Wave." CNN, October 27, 2009, http://edition.cnn.com/2009/TECH/10/27/rasmussen.brothers.google.wave (December 13, 2014).

Tannenbaum, Rob, and Craig Marks. *I Want My MTV: The Uncensored Story of the Music Video Revolution.* New York: Plume, 2012.

Tapia, Andrea Hoplight. "Techno-Armageddon: The Millennial Christian Response to Y2K." *Review of Religious Research* 43, no. 3 (2002): 266–86.

Taussig, Michael. *Mimesis and Alterity: A Particular History of the Senses.* New York: Routledge, 1993.

Teinowitz, Ira. "Bud Dry Pitches Women." *Advertising Age,* July 1, 1991, 10.

Tenner, Edward. "Chronologically Incorrect." *Wilson Quarterly* 22, no. 4 (autumn, 1998): 27–37.

"The Postman." Box Office Mojo, http://www.boxofficemojo.com/movies/?id=postman htm (December 19, 2013).

The Room. Directed by Tommy Wiseau. 2003; Los Angeles: Wiseau-Films, 2005. DVD.

Thompson, Chris. "Vince McMahon May Be Reviving The XFL." *Deadspin,* December 17, 2017, https://deadspin.com/vince-mcmahon-may-be-reviving-the-failed- xfl-1821354064 (December 20, 2017).

Tilley, Christopher, ed. *Reading Material Culture: Structuralism, Hermeneutics and Post- Structuralism.* Cambridge, MA: Basil Blackwell, 1991.

Trapani, Gina. "On Google Wave and 'Failed' Experiments." *SmarterWare,* August 5, 2010, http://smarterware.org/6499/on-google-wave-and-failed-experiments (Decem- ber 12, 2014).

Troll 2. Directed by Claudio Fragasso. 1991; Beverly Hills, CA: Twentieth Century Fox Home Entertainment, 2010. DVD.

"Troll 2 (1990)." Rotten Tomatoes. http://www.rottentomatoes.com/m/troll-2 (Decem- ber 12, 2013).

"UK Drive to Beat Y2K Panic." BBC News, June 8, 1999, http://news.bbc.co.uk/2/hi/uk_news/363761.stm (December 2, 2014).

The Vandals. "I've Got an Ape Drape." *Hitler Bad, Vandals Good.* Nitro Records, 1998, compact disc.

Vardy, Jill, and Chris Wattie. "Shopping Is Patriotic, Leaders Say." *National Post* (Canada), September 28, 2001.

Veblen, Thorstein. *The Theory of the Leisure Class: An Economic Study of Institutions.* New York: Mentor Books, 1953.

Wahl, Melissa. "Worries over Y2K Bug a Waste, Bankers Stress." *Chicago Tribune,* July 25, 1999, http://articles.chicagotribune.com/1999-07-25/business/9907250112_1_pinnacle-bank-y2k-ellen-seidman (February 15, 2013).

Wald, Matthew L. "FAA Faulted on Fixing Year 2000 Computer Glitch." *New York Times,* February 4, 1998, http://www.nytimes.com/1998/02/04/us/faa-faulted-on-fixing-year-2000-computer-glitch.html (January 12, 2014).

Waterworld. Directed by Kevin Costner and Kevin Reynolds. 1995; Hollywood, CA: Universal Studios, 1997. DVD.

"Waterworld." Rotten Tomatoes. http://www.rottentomatoes.com/m/waterworld (December 19, 2013).

Watkins, Gwynne. "Forget the Walkman, Can 'Guardians of the Galaxy Vol. 2' Make the Zune Cool?" *Yahoo! Movies,* last modified May 11, 2017, https://www.yahoo.com/movies/can-guardians-galaxy-vol-2-finally-make-zune-cool-174550564.html (June 25, 2017).

"Welcome to Rate My Mullet.com!" RateMyMullet.com. http://www.ratemymullet.com/?page=home (June 30, 2012).

West, Candace, and Don Zimmerman. "Doing Gender." *Gender and Society* 1, no. 2 (June 1987): 125–51.

"White House Seeks to Dispel Y2K Panic." *Los Angeles Times,* December 13, 1999, http://articles.latimes.com/1999/dec/13/news/mn-43438 (December 12, 2014).

"Why Did the iPod Succeed While the Zune Failed?" Quora.com, 2012, https://www.quora.com/Why-did-the-iPod-succeed-while-the-Zune-failed (June 12, 2017).

Williams, Martyn. "Computer Problems Hit Three Nuclear Plants in Japan." CNN, January 3, 2000, http://archives.cnn.com/2000/TECH/computing/01/03/japan.nukes.y2k.idg (January 12, 2013).

Williams, Raymond. *The Sociology of Culture.* New York: Shocken Books, 1981.

Woodward, Ian. *Understanding Material Culture.* Thousand Oaks, CA: Sage, 2009.

"XFL Post-Game Conference." NBC Sports, February 3, 2001, https://www.youtube.com/watch?v=f45h11D0Wwk (February 7, 2018).

Zakarin, Jordon. "Vanilla Ice on Real Estate, DIY Show and How He Got That Name." *Huffington Post,* August 2, 2011, http://www.huffingtonpost.com/2011/06/02/vanilla-ice-talks-diy-show-name_n_870170.html (July 12, 2012).

Zubaz. "About." http://www.zubaz.com/pages/about_us (June 18, 2014).

Index

About the Author

Salvador Jimenez Murguía is associate professor of sociology at Akita International University. His research interests include racism, failure, and deviant behavior and popular culture. He is the editor of *The Encyclopedia of Japanese Horror Films* (2016) and *The Encyclopedia of Racism in American Films* (2018), and the coeditor of *The Encyclopedia of Contemporary Spanish Films* (2018), all published by Rowman & Littlefield.

Lightning Source UK Ltd.
Milton Keynes UK
UKHW01n0034070918
328436UK00001B/33/P